CB Radio
Servicing Guide

by Leo G. Sands

HOWARD W. SAMS & CO., INC.

THE BOBBS-MERRILL COMPANY, INC.

Indianapolis • New York

FIRST EDITION

FIRST PRINTING—MARCH, 1963

CB RADIO SERVICING GUIDE

Preface

The tremendous growth of Citizens band radio in the last five years has far outstripped the service facilities of the manufacturer and technician alike. And as the number of CB units in service has increased, so has the demand for maintenance.

Thus, the opportunity for radio and TV service shops to expand into CB service has never been better. There are many radio and TV service technicians who already have the Second-Class Radiotelephone Operator's license needed to perform or supervise *complete* maintenance of CB radio units, although no license is needed for the great majority of CB radio service calls. The technically inclined nonprofessional need have no qualms on this score.

This book was written to furnish a comprehensive guide to CB radio servicing—to aid not only the professional service technician, but also the CB radio user who wishes to repair his own set. A troubleshooting chart, covering most of the common CB unit troubles, has been included, in addition to numerous other diagrams and tables describing CB radio operation. It is felt that by using this guide in conjunction with the details furnished in manufacturer's manuals, complete CB radio maintenance can be accomplished quickly and easily.

LEO G. SANDS

February, 1963

Table of Contents

Chapter 1

Chapter 2

Chapter 3

Chapter 4

Chapter 5

Chapter 6

Chapter 7

Chapter 8

Chapter 9

Citizens Band Radio Equipment

A Citizens band radio, or CB set, is usually considered as a radio transmitter-receiver, or transceiver, which is capable of operation on one or more of the 23 channel frequencies in the so-called Citizens band between 26.965 and 27.255 megacycles (mc). It is used for two-way radiotelephone communications on a simplex basis (transmission and reception take place sequentially, not simultaneously). It employs amplitude modulation (AM), and transmitter power is limited to 5 watts input, 3.5 watts output. Single-sideband transmission is also permitted. A Class-D radio-station license is required in order to use the transmitter; however, no operator license is required.

DEFINITIONS AND RULES

There are other classes of equipment which are also licensed in the Citizens Radio Service. These include Class-C radio-control transmitters, which operate in the same band, and Class-A and Class-B stations which operate in the 460-470-mc UHF band. This book covers only equipment intended to be licensed as a Class-D Citizens Radio station.

All Class-D Citizens Radio stations are classified in the license as mobile units, whether used at fixed locations, on board conveyances, or carried from place to place.

The transmitters of all Class-D Citizens Radio units are crystal-controlled, as required by FCC regulations. The receivers may be fixed-tuned or tunable across the band. The following general types of CB sets are currently on the market:

1. Single-channel, fixed-tuned transmitter-receiver,
2. Single-channel, fixed-tuned transmitter, tunable receiver,
3. Multiselectable-channel transmitter-receiver,
4. Multiselectable-channel transmitter, tunable receiver,

Courtesy Heath Co.
(A) Single-channel transmit-receive unit.

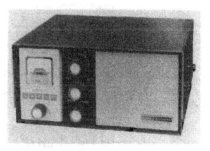

Courtesy Kaar Engineering Corp.
(B) Five-channel transmitter, tunable receiver.

(C) Eight crystal-controlled transmit-receive channels; all-channel tunable receiver.

Courtesy Lafayette Radio Electronics Corp.
Fig. 1-1. Representative CB transceivers.

5. Same as No. 3, but also has integral facilities for AM broadcast-band reception,
6. 23-selectable-channel transmitter, tunable receiver,
7. 23-selectable-channel transmitter-receiver.

Examples of various types of sets are shown in Fig. 1-1.

Some CB sets are designed for operation only from a 115-volt, 60-cycle AC source. When used on conveyances, an external DC power pack is required, or an external DC-to-AC inverter is employed to convert available DC to AC.

Most CB sets now on the market are designed to operate from either 12 volts DC or 115 volts AC without requiring modification, while some are designed to operate from 6 or 12 volts DC or 115 volts AC.

Base Station

A base station (licensed as a mobile unit) is a transmitter-receiver installed at a fixed location and used primarily for communicating with mobile and portable stations. A base station is generally connected to an outside antenna. For short-range communication (a mile or so) an indoor antenna can be used.

Fixed Station

A fixed station is one that is used only for communicating with other stations at fixed locations. A station at a fixed location, which is used to communicate with mobile units as well as other stations at fixed locations, is classed as a base station.

Mobile Station

While all Class-D CB stations are classed as mobile units in the station license, the trade refers to mobile units as mobile or transportable stations. A mobile station may be either temporarily or permanently installed in a vehicle.

Portable Stations

A portable station may be a hand-held walkie-talkie or a type as shown in Fig. 1-2. Walkie-talkies, which are operated

Fig. 1-2. Portable transceiver.

Courtesy Vocaline Co. of America

under Part 15, FCC Rules and Regulations, as low-power communications devices, need not be licensed. However, when they are used for communicating with licensed Class-D stations, walkie-talkies must be licensed and must meet the technical requirements of Part 19 of the FCC rules.

TECHNICAL AND OPERATIONAL DATA

Class-D CB transmitters may employ AM (A3) or SSB (A3a) types of modulation. Power input to the final RF stage is limited to 5 watts, output to 3.5 watts. Transmitter frequency stability must be 0.005% or better. Highest permitted

9

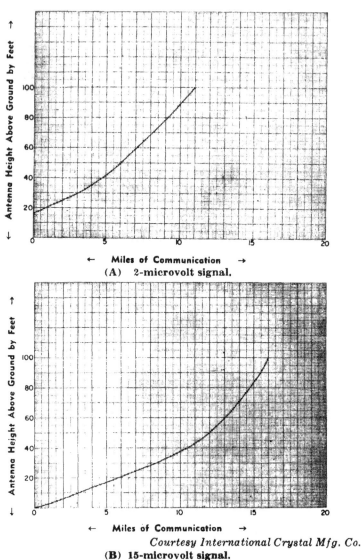

(A)   2-microvolt signal.

Courtesy International Crystal Mfg. Co.

(B) 15-microvolt signal.

Fig. 1-3. Range using ground plane or coaxial antenna.

modulation frequency is 3,000 cps. Antenna elevation is limited to 20 feet above an existing structure, as defined in FCC Rules and Regulations, Part 19.

A Class-D CB transmitter may not be remote-controlled; nor can CB transmissions be rebroadcast over a public address system. A CB station may not be patched into a tele-

10

phone line. Class-D CB stations may not be used for long distance skip communication, however, communication between stations within 150 miles of each other is permitted.

Communicating range under these restrictions normally is limited to about 1 mile between two fixed stations equipped with indoor antennas. When an outdoor antenna is used at both fixed stations, distances of 20 miles can sometimes be spanned. The range of base-to-mobile communications depends on the effective elevation of the base-station antenna and the elevation of the ground where the mobile unit is operating, as well as terrain conditions between the stations. Range is also limited by the noise conditions at both locations.

The purchaser of a CB system should not expect to enjoy the same range and relative freedom from noise and interference from other stations as users of higher-powered commercial FM mobile equipment. Base-to-mobile range of 5 miles may be maximum in many cases. Under some (exceptional) conditions, a 10 to 20 mile range is enjoyed.

The graphs shown in Fig. 1-3 indicate the calculated ranges to be anticipated under various conditions. While a receiver, under shop bench-test conditions, may be sensitive to signals of less than 1 microvolt, noise conditions in actual use may be such that a 15-microvolt signal is required for useful communications. The CB hobbyist will often tolerate reception conditions which are totally unsatisfactory to the business user of CB radio.

WHO CAN SERVICE CB SETS?

The FCC has no jurisdiction over radio receivers, except when they radiate radio signals (generally from a local oscillator) in excess of limits specified in Part 15 of its rules. The commission does control the use of radio transmitters of all types and requires a station license for operation of transmitters, except when power is under the values specified in Part 15.

A transmitter may be repaired or adjusted by anyone as long as it is not connected to an antenna and does not radiate a signal. But, when connected to an antenna, it must be licensed (except as permitted in Part 15) and if it operates in an unlawful manner, the station licensee is responsible.

A radio operator license is required by persons, or supervisors of persons, who make any repairs or adjustments to a transmitter which could cause it to operate in an unlawful manner, when connected to a radiating antenna. An unlicensed person can make such repairs or adjustments, but the transmitter should be checked out by a licensed operator, or under his supervision, before it is put on the air.

No operator license is required to perform the following in connection with CB sets, even when connected to a radiating antenna.

1. Measure transmitter frequency.
2. Measure modulation level.
3. Tune transmitter-output circuit.
4. Replace tubes or vibrator.
5. Re-align receiver.
6. Replace components, except in transmitter oscillator circuit or any components which could cause over-modulation.
7. Replace receiver crystals.
8. Install or replace antenna system.

An operator license is required by persons (or their supervisor) who perform any of the following:

1. Replace transmitter crystals.
2. Trim oscillator frequency (in sets with crystal padder).
3. Replace oscillator-circuit components, except tube of same type as original.
4. Modify transmitter circuitry.

To service CB equipment, technicians who perform the above tasks are required to possess either a First-Class or Second-Class Radiotelephone Operator License. There is no fee for a license, but the applicant must pass a written test on electronic fundamentals and radio regulations.

CUSTOMER COMPLAINTS

The most common complaints made by customers include excessive noise, inadequate range and channel congestion. Many times this is because the purchaser of CB equipment has been oversold. It then becomes the serviceman's chore to educate the customer. Citizens Radio can be very useful if correctly installed and used, and when it is used for its intended purpose—short-range, two-way radio communication.

Excessive Noise

Noisy reception is caused mostly by the electrical systems of motor vehicles. The noise generated by the customer's own vehicle can be suppressed. But radiation of noise generated by other nearby vehicles cannot be stopped until laws are enacted that will require all vehicles to be treated to minimize radiation of electrical interference. Noise from nearby vehicles is reduced in CB sets that are equipped with noise limiters or noise blankers, but it is not totally eliminated. Noise can be minimized by increasing the strength of the received signal so that it will override the noise. This is done by improving either the receiving or transmitting system of the station being received.

Electrical noise generated in a vehicle is sometimes picked up by the transmitter and associated wiring and modulates the transmitted signal. If the signal from a mobile unit is accompanied by noise and the same noise is not heard when there is no signal (receiver fully unsquelched), this could be the cause.

Transmitting System Improvements—The transmitting system can be improved by feeding more power into the antenna and by locating the antenna more advantageously. Transmitter power output is limited to 3.5 watts, which is greater than the continuous capability of most CB transmitters. Effective transmitter power output can be raised by modulating the transmitter more heavily. If the microphone is used incorrectly (too far from mouth), modulation will be low. If used correctly, a higher level of modulation and consequently greater power output will be realized. Customers should be taught correct microphone techniques.

Low line voltage can reduce transmitter power. If the AC line voltage at the customer's installation is less than 115 volts, it can be boosted with a transformer. Low battery voltage in a car calls for replacement of a defective battery or adjustment of the voltage regulator by an auto electrician (not a radio man).

Although the height of a CB base-station antenna is limited by FCC regulations to 20 feet above an existing structure, sometimes the highest lawful location is not the best spot. Trial and error location techniques might be required. Also, in cases of unsatisfactory power radiation, the antenna itself may be at fault. If it does not closely match the impedance of the transmission line (coaxial cable), too much of the power is reflected back to the transmitter and not radiated into space. The coaxial cable, if more than 50 feet long, may sap too much of the available power. Replacement with lower-loss cable will increase the effective radiated power.

Receiving System Improvements—Noisy reception is seldom due to lack of receiver sensitivity. A typical CB receiver will pick up signals with a field strength of 3 microvolts per meter or less; unfortunately, the noise picked up by the antenna is often greater than that. Hence, the typical CB receiver has greater sensitivity than can be effectively utilized. The trick is to improve the signal pick-up of the antenna and to suppress the generation of electrical noise in the vicinity of the receiver.

In a vehicular installation the first step is to install noise suppressors (described later). Another step is to place the antenna in the most advantageous location. In the center of the metal car top is the best place, but most customers won't let you put it there.

At the base station, the antenna should be located as far away as possible from sources of noise, but not so far that an excessively long coaxial cable is required. Noise generated by electric motors, aquarium thermostats, and switches should be suppressed with suitable filters.

Inadequate Range

Inadequate range is a term that is often misinterpreted. The customer may expect more range than his equipment can deliver under the circumstances peculiar to his locations and environment. Maximum attainable range may not be realized because of excessive noise, which is not the fault of the equipment, or because of improper use (wrong microphone technique), less-than-optimum antenna systems, or improperly operating equipment.

High noise level when no signal is present generally indicates that the receiver is sensitive. However, if a receiver crystal is off-frequency, the receiver may not be sufficiently sensitive to on-frequency signals. By the same token, a signal from an off-frequency transmitter will not be as well received by an on-frequency receiver. If the receiver does not have a noise limiter, its useful receiving range may be impaired. Noise-limiter kits are available which can be added to existing receivers.

Channel Congestion

When a customer finds that he is operating on an overly congested channel, the simplest cure is to change the operating frequency. In the case of a single-channel set, new crystals are required. Crystals can be added to multichannel sets so that the customer will have a choice of channels.

If the customer has a 23-channel set, he can determine which channel is least congested by monitoring and then operate on that frequency.

14

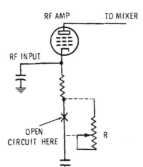

Fig. 1-4. Adding RF gain control to receiver.

Sometimes, apparent congestion is caused by strong signals on an adjacent channel. Few CB sets are selective enough to reject very strong adjacent-channel signals. Sometimes, strong adjacent-channel signals will desensitize a receiver by over-loading its front end or causing an increase in AVC voltage. This can be minimized by adding an RF gain control to the receiver, as shown in Fig. 1-4, if the receiver has an RF amplifier stage. The cathode circuit is opened as shown and a potentiometer is added. The resistance of the potentiometer may range from 1,000 ohms to 5,000 ohms, depending on the type of tube used. The potentiometer is set so that the receiver has only adequate sensitivity for the intended purpose.

TONE SQUELCH

The receiver can be silenced at all times, except to intercept signals from desired stations, if all stations in a system are equipped with tone squelch. Whenever a transmitter is turned on, an audio tone is transmitted (tone-squelch encoder

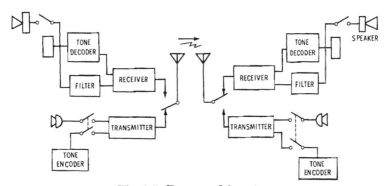

Fig. 1-5. Tone-squelch system.

15

modulates transmitter) which unlocks the tone squelch decoder of all associated receivers. The tone may be at such a low frequency that it is not objectionable, or it may be filtered out at each associated receiver, as shown in Fig. 1-5. It will then be inaudible at associated receivers but will be heard at all receivers within range which do not have tone-squelch decoders. Voice is transmitted over the tone.

Tone-squelch kits and adaptors are available with built-in tone squelch. While tone squelch locks out receivers until a signal is intercepted which is modulated by a tone of appropriate frequency, it will not lock out non-tone-accompanied signals while the unlocking tone is being received.

SELECTIVE SIGNALING

Some customers may want to be able to call their associated receivers selectively, without alerting others. One of the earliest commercial mobile radio selective signaling systems, introduced by Hammarlund in 1947, utilized audio tones of various frequencies. Each receiver was equipped with a tone decoder that turned on the speaker when a specific combination of tones was received. Selection was made at the transmitter by means of pushbuttons. Several manufacturers now offer similar devices that can be added to CB sets.

Stations can be signaled selectively by means of a telephone dial which causes tone pulses to be transmitted. These pulses are counted at the receiver by an electromechanical selector. One of the earliest dial-signaling systems, introduced by Link Radio Corporation, employed stepping relays to decode pulses. Most widely used today is the Secode dial system which employs an electromechanical selector (Fig. 1-6) that can be set to respond to any one of more than 300,000 dialed numbers. Some other systems employ an AP-60 selector which is alternately keyed by two tones.

Fig. 1-6. Pulse decoder.

Courtesy Secode Corp.

16

Fig. 1-7. Multiple tone encoder.

Courtesy Motorola Communications and Electronics, Inc.

Most of the multiple-tone-type (frequency division) selective-signaling systems now on the market employ resonant reeds to generate tones and vibrating-reed relays to decode tone signals. A typical base-station encoder is shown in Fig. 1-7. They are relatively inexpensive and are faster to use (pushbuttons) than dial-type systems—but they have smaller capacity. Like tone squelch, selective signaling locks out receivers until the correct code is received, but it does not prevent reception of unwanted stations during the time the receiver is unlocked.

Chapter 2

Test Equipment

It is possible for an experienced technician to service CB sets with a minimum of tools. A neon-lamp-type line checker, a No. 47 pilot lamp, and a few hand tools will sometimes suffice. However, to do a professional job, adequate test equipment is required.

FIELD SERVICE EQUIPMENT

For field service calls, the following equipment is essential: through-line RF power meter, tube tester, volt-ohm-milliam-meter, and frequency meter. Field servicing is generally confined to correction of faults which do not require replacement of other than plug-in components. If other trouble exists in the CB set, it should be taken to the shop for repair.

The through-line-type RF power meter (Fig. 2-1) is essential for determining whether the trouble is in the transmitter, microphone, or antenna system. A portable tube tester

Fig. 2-1. Portable through-line type RF power meter.

Courtesy Seco Mfg. Co.

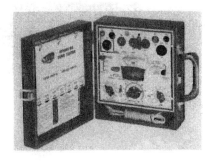

Fig. 2-2. Tube tester which
measures merit and grid emission.

Courtesy Seco Mfg. Co.

(Fig. 2-2) is an obvious necessity, and a VOM (volt-ohm-milliammeter) is handy to have along for measuring AC line voltage (or battery voltage).

Since the customer is responsible to the FCC for the proper operation of his transmitter and because off-frequency operation is the most common technical violation of FCC rules, an accurate frequency meter (Fig. 2-3) should always be available for checking transmitter frequencies.

SHOP EQUIPMENT

The shop requires a more extensive array of test equipment, including the following:

1. Dummy antenna loads,
2. RF power meter,
3. Tube tester, dynamic mutual-conductance type capable of checking for grid emission,

Fig. 2-3. Direct-reading
frequency meter.

Courtesy Hammarlund Mfg. Co.

19

4. Volt-ohm-milliammeter,
5. Frequency meter, accurate to *at least* 0.0025%, tunable to all 23 Class-D CB channels,
6. Vacuum-tube-voltmeter,
7. RF probe,
8. Signal generator,
9. Grid-dip meter,
10. Oscilloscope,
11. Capacitor checker,
12. Transistor tester,
13. 6/12-volt power source,
14. Variable AC-voltage source,
15. Set of coaxial plug adaptors.

In addition, a 23-channel (crystal-controlled transmit and receive) CB set makes it easier to check out other CB sets.

Dummy Antenna Load

No transmitter should be serviced when connected to a radiating antenna, because harmful interference can be caused to others. A radiating antenna should be used only when it is known that the transmitter will operate in conformity with applicable FCC technical standards, and when the transmitter and operator are covered by a valid station license. All transmitter servicing in the shop should be performed only when the transmitter is terminated in a nonradiating dummy load or loaded-type RF power meter.

The simplest dummy load consists of a No. 47 pilot lamp, as shown in Fig. 2-4. A variety of these dummy loads should

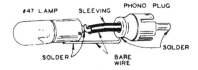

Fig. 2-4. Lamp-type dummy load.

Courtesy Heath Co.

be available to fit every type of antenna plug required for all makes of CB sets to be serviced. The lamp serves as a load (approximately 50 ohms) and as a relative power-output and modulation indicator.

A dummy load, that more accurately approximates 50 ohms, is shown in Fig. 2-5. The RF power and modulation meter shown in Fig. 2-6 contains a dummy load as well as a meter, rectifiers, and other components for measuring power and modulation level. Its dummy load (Fig. 2-7) consists of two

20

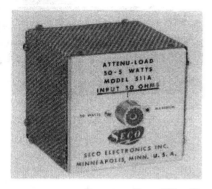

Fig. 2-5. Dummy load, an essential
servicing tool.

Courtesy Seco Mfg. Co.

18-ohm (R1 and R2) and a 15-ohm resistor connected in
series. The meter measures rectified RF current, and its scale
is calibrated in milliamperes and watts.

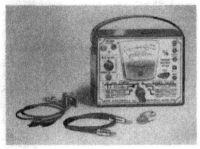

Fig. 2-6. Combination RF power
and modulation meter.

Courtesy Seco Mfg. Co.

RF Power Meter

The RF power meter shown in Fig. 2-8 requires an external
dummy load. It is intended for connection between an
antenna and a transmitter or between an antenna and a
dummy load.

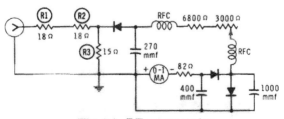

Fig. 2-7. RF power meter.

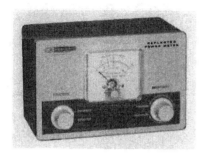

Fig. 2-8. RF power meter for
transmitter tune up and antenna-
efficiency measurement.

Courtesy Heath Co.

A schematic of a similar instrument is shown in Fig. 2-9. The signal from the transmitter is passed through a directional coupler, a piece of transmission line within the instrument, to the antenna or dummy load. In this particular instrument, J1 and J2 are connected by a hollow metal rod. On each side of, and parallel to this metal rod are two pieces of wire whose opposing ends are connected alternately by S1 to a rectifier and a meter. The combination of inductive and capacitive coupling is such that the incident RF voltage on the line is balanced out, and the reflected power (returning from the antenna or dummy load) can be measured. The switch can be set to read either incident or reflected power. Incident power is the power that is delivered by the transmitter. Reflected power is the power reflected back to the transmitter because of mismatch. The difference between these two measurements can be translated into terms of SWR (standing wave ratio) or efficiency.

This kind of RF power meter is more flexible than the loaded or absorption-type RF power meter since it can be used in the shop with a dummy load or in the field to measure antenna efficiency.

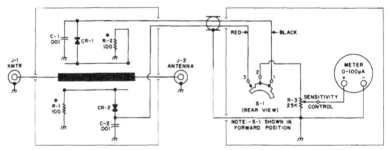

* FOR 72 Ω LINE. FOR 52 Ω LINES, R1 AND R2 = 160 Ω RESISTORS.

Courtesy Allied Radio Corp.

Fig. 2-9. Schematic diagram of through-line type of RF power meter.

Field-Strength Meter

Field-strength (FS) meters are useful in the shop as well as in the field. Even when a dummy load is used, enough RF is radiated in the vicinity of the CB set to get an indication on an FS meter. A simple field-strength meter (Fig. 2-10)

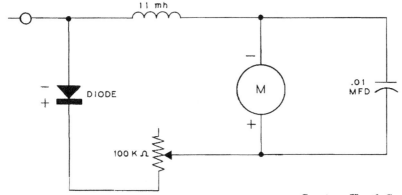

Courtesy Heath Co.

Fig. 2-10. Simple field-strength meter.

consists of a DC microammeter or milliammeter which measures rectified RF current. A short piece of wire connected to the terminal at the upper left suffices as an antenna at short range.

A more sensitive FS meter, in addition to a diode detector, will contain a transistor amplifier whose collector current is measured by the meter.

Tube Testers

There are many tube testers on the market; and various claims are made for the different measuring techniques used. The simplest measure cathode emission. More elaborate tube testers measure dynamic mutual conductance. The difference among tube testers is in their ability to detect tube defects. Highly critical tube testers are expensive and generally more difficult to operate. A tube tester is an essential tool, regardless of its type, for culling out tubes that are shorted or weak. One tube fault that is not readily detected by all types of tube testers is grid emission. Some testers, however, are designed to check for this fault, because it is a major cause of equipment instability. Defective tubes which pass muster on a tube tester occasionally make themselves obvious by the manner in which they perform in the set.

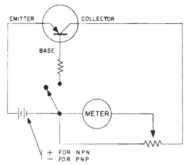

Fig. 2-11. DC-type transistor checker.

Courtesy Allied Radio Corp.

Transistor Testers

While few CB sets employ transistors, the CB shop should be prepared to test them. The simplest type of transistor checker will detect excessive leakage and measure gain. Leakage current is measured with the transistor base disconnected, as shown in Fig. 2-11, and gain is measured by noting the increase in meter reading when S1 is closed to apply forward bias to the transistor base.

The dynamic-type transistor checker shown in Fig. 2-12 can be used to check most transistors without removing them from the set. By means of clip leads the transistor is connected into

Courtesy Seco Mfg. Co.
Fig. 2-12. In-circuit type transistor tester.

24

an oscillator circuit. Oscillator output is detected by a neon lamp. Transistor merit is determined by adjustment of the base current control and noting the reading at the point where oscillation ceases.

Also available are more elaborate bench-type transistor checkers, which measure gain, leakage current, and (by calculation) other performance characteristics. Switches are usually provided for setting DC voltages to the required levels for different types of transistors and diodes.

Frequency Meters

The most important CB servicing instrument is a frequency meter. It must have an accuracy of at least ±0.0025% to measure CB transmitter frequencies with sufficient accuracy. CB Class-D transmitters must remain within 0.005% of their stated frequency.

Heterodyne frequency meter—Frequency meters suitable for CB servicing range in cost from a little above $200 to $1,000, or more. One type is tunable to any frequency in the band. It consists of a variable frequency oscillator (Fig. 2-13)

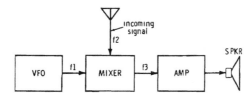

Fig. 2-13. Block diagram of heterodyne frequency meter.

whose output signal (f1) is mixed with the signal (f2) of the transmitter being checked. When the two signals are not exactly at the same frequency, the resulting beat frequency (f3) is fed into the amplifier and then to a speaker to headphones to make it audible. The frequency-meter dial (VFO tuning) is adjusted for zero beat and the dial reading is referenced to a calibration curve. Or, if the transmitter frequency can be trimmed, the frequency meter is set to the desired frequency and the transmitter frequency trimmed until zero beat is obtained.

Heterodyne-type frequency meters have the advantage that they can be tuned to any frequency within their range, generally without any modification or addition of accessories. Some contain one or more built-in frequency-reference crys-

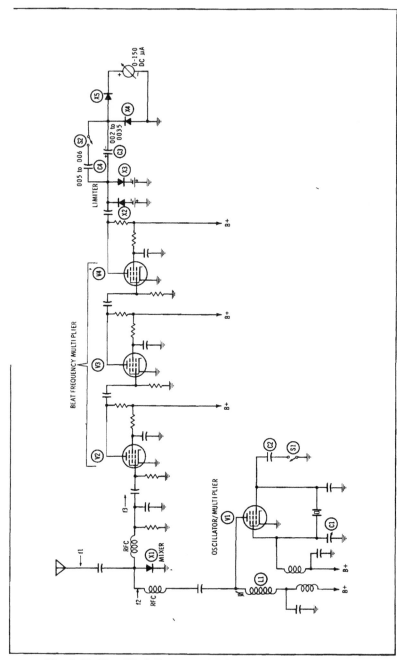

Fig. 2-14. Simplified diagram of difference frequency meter.

26

tals for checking VFO calibration. Such instruments should be checked against WWV or other frequency standard at regular intervals.

The accuracy of measurements made with a heterodyne-type frequency meter depends on the following factors:

1. The accuracy of the instrument,
2. The accuracy with which the instrument dial is read by the user,
3. The accuracy with which the dial reading is interpreted from the calibration curve.

One manufacturer has reduced the human-error factor by furnishing a Citizens-band frequency-reference table with its heterodyne-type frequency meter. Each instrument is tested at all 23 CB-channels frequencies, and the meter-dial readings for each channel are listed in the reference table. The user merely looks up the channel setting on the table instead of on a calibration curve.

Direct-reading frequency meter—Another basic type of frequency meter in wide use is the so-called "difference" type. It compares the frequency of the transmitter with a known fixed frequency and measures the difference.

The transmitter signal (f1) picked up by the frequency-meter atenna is fed through a small capacitor to a crystal detector, mixer diode X1, as shown in Fig. 2-14. Reference signal f2 from oscillator V1 is also fed to X1 and is heterodyned with f1. If there is any difference in their frequencies, a beat note (f3) is produced which is amplified about 55 db by V2, V3, and V4. Beat signal f3 is then passed through full-wave diode limiter X2-X3 which converts f3 into a square wave. The square wave is then passed through a capacitor to full-wave rectifier X4 and X5. The resulting DC voltage measured by the meter is translated into terms of frequency.

The crystal oscillator operates at a submultiple of f2. L1, the plate tank of V1, is tuned to the crystal second harmonic. This signal is further multiplied in frequency by diode X1. To measure a frequency of 27.025 mc, a crystal which oscillates at 6,756.25 kc is used. Capacitor C1 is adjusted at the factory to set the crystal exactly on the desired frequency. L1 is tuned to 13,512.5 kc, the crystal second harmonic. Various harmonics of 13,512.5 kc are generated by X1, but the second harmonic (fourth harmonic of crystal) 27,025 mc, is the only one that produces a suitable beat signal (f3 within ±15 kc of 27.025 mc) when mixed with an incoming signal.

If the incoming signal is at 27.026 mc, f3 will be 1 kc (1,000 cps). This 1,000-cps signal is amplified and converted into square wave pulses which, when counted, causes the meter to indicate a 1-kc deviation from the reference frequency.

The user now knows that the transmitter frequency is 1 kc off, but does not know if it is 1 kc higher or lower than the reference frequency. This is determined by momentarily closing S1, lowering the frequency of the reference oscillator. If the meter reading increases when S1 is closed, the transmitter frequency is on the high side; and on the low side, if the meter reading decreases.

The meter is a 0-150 DC microammeter with an internal resistance of 500 ohms; it has a 0-50/150 scale. When S2 is open, the 0-50 scale is used to measure frequency deviation up to 5 kc. When S2 is closed, the 0-150 scale indicates deviation up to 15 kc.

The frequency of beat signal f3 is measured by a positive counting circuit. When a positive square-wave pulse is applied to C3, X5 conducts, and current flows through the meter until C3 is charged in the polarity indicated in the diagram. When the square-wave signal swings negative, X4 conducts, discharging C3 and recharging it in the opposite polarity. With each succeeding positive pulse, current flows through the meter until C3 is charged. The current through the meter increases as pulse repetition rate f3 increases, and vice versa. In the circuit shown, the value of C3 is such that a 5-kc square wave causes the meter current to be 50 microamperes. When S2 is closed, C4 is paralleled across C3 and the meter indicates full scale when f3 is 15 kc. The values of C3 and C4 indicated on the diagram are approximate and are selected at the factory when the instrument is calibrated.

In the actual multichannel frequency meter, a selector switch is used for selecting a separate crystal for each frequency. While the circuit shown employs tubes, solid-state circuitry has recently become more common in instruments of this type.

Several frequency meters are on the market, including those made by Budelman, International Crystal, DuMont, and Hammarlund. One of the newest ones is the Hammarlund TM-48A; it has capacity for measuring up to 48 frequencies. For CB servicing, only 23 RF channel crystals need be installed. Additional crystals may be added for IF's of receivers to be serviced for reasons to be explained later.

The kind of frequency meter to buy depends on your budget and the scope of the work to be performed. For CB work only, a continuously tunable heterodyne-type frequency meter with an accuracy of 0.0025% or a difference-type instrument

28

equipped with 0.0025% accuracy crystals for each channel to be measured will suffice.

However, if you plan to service commercial mobile-radio equipment also, you will need a frequency meter with an accuracy of at least ±0.00025%, since 152-74-mc and 450-470-mc band equipment frequency tolerance is ± 0.0005%. A difference-type frequency meter with capacity for 48 channels can be equipped with crystals for all 23 CB channels as well as for many commercial mobile channels.

Signal Generators

One of the handiest CB servicing tools is an all-frequency signal generator. They are generally packaged like a fountain pen and contain a multivibrator whose output signal is rich in harmonics and requires no tuning. When its probe is touched to the antenna jack or grid of almost any stage in a receiver, an audio tone is heard in the speaker, if the set is functioning.

A tunable RF signal generator is required for alignment of receiver IF and RF circuits. It must be tunable to all of the intermediate frequencies (IF) of the receivers to be serviced (262.5 kc to 10.7 mc), and through the Citizens band (26.96-27.23 mc).

There is a wide selection from which to choose. Many low-priced signal generators, are available, covering frequencies from below 262.5 kc to 30 mc or higher. While nearly all signal generators will produce a signal at the required frequencies, not all are satisfactory for CB servicing.

It is important that the signal generator be accurately calibrated and possess high-frequency stability. Typically, the calibration accuracy is 2%, which means that at 262.5 kc the frequency error could be as great as 5.25 kc, and at 27.025 mc, the error could be as great as 540.5 kc, which is more than half a megacycle. This is considerable since the Citizens band is only 290-kc wide.

More expensive laboratory-grade signal generators are typically rated at 1% accuracy, which is some improvement,

Fig. 2-15. Kit-type signal generator
capable of covering IF and
CB frequencies.

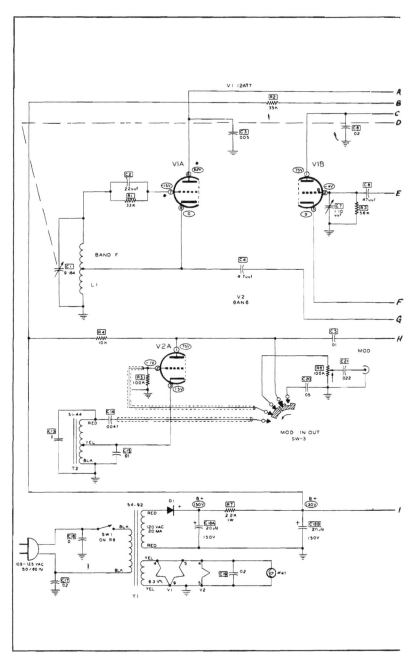

Fig. 2-16. Signal generator diagram—note dual

30

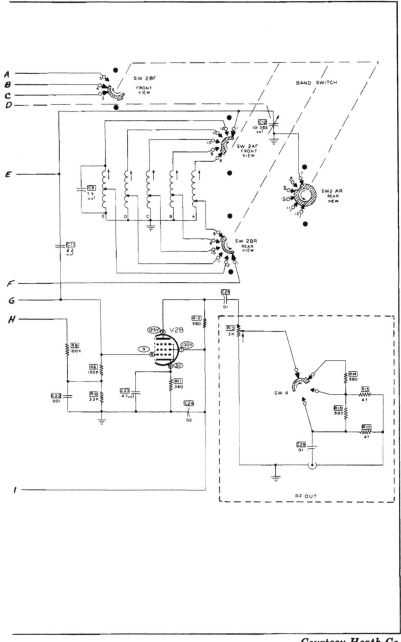

attenuator circuit in lower right corner.

but not enough to permit use of a signal generator as a frequency standard. Since it is often necessary to be able to set a signal generator to the desired frequency with great accuracy, an external frequency standard can be of great value.

For setting a signal generator accurately to an IF, such as 262.5 kc, 455 kc, or 1,650 kc, etc., a military surplus BC-221 frequency meter can be used. The BC-221 covers the 100-20,000-kc range, and is available from many sources at bargain prices.

For setting a signal generator *fairly* accurately to one of the CB channels, an incoming signal can be used as a reference. However, a frequency meter is much better for this purpose, because of the possibility that the incoming signal may be off frequency.

Attenuators—Another requirement of a signal generator is the ability to attenuate its output to less than 1 microvolt. While the dials on a low-cost signal generator might indicate that the output is set for 1 microvolt, due to inadequate shielding there may be so much signal leakage past the attenuator and through the case that the signal reaching the receiver may be considerably stronger.

There are, however, several signal generators on the market that are adequate for CB servicing. The one shown in Fig. 2-15, available in kit form, is tunable from 100 kc to 110 mc and contains an internal audio-tone modulator. It can also be modulated by an external audio-signal generator. It has two RF output attenuators—coarse and fine. The attenuator circuits are shown in Fig. 2-16 inside the dotted line area. Coarse large-step attenuation is controlled by switch SW-4, and fine, continuous attenuation is controlled by potentiometer R13.

Frequency meter as signal generator—A frequency meter is often used as a signal generator because of its known frequency accuracy. Some are equipped with an RF output jack to permit direct connection to a receiver, and with an attenuator to vary the RF output. When not equipped with an RF output jack, the signal is picked up by placing the frequency meter, or its pick-up antenna, as close to the receiver as necessary.

Specifications—To make receiver performance tests, the signal generator must have the following basic characteristics:

Frequency range	260 kc to 30 mc
Frequency accuracy	2% or better
Modulation	30% AM
RF output range	0.5-100,000 microvolts

Wave Analyzers

Another instrument that is being used more widely, but is not an essential, is a wave analyzer or distortion meter. It is required for making SINAD receiver sensitivity measurements, and useful for measuring modulation and audio receiving distortion. These instruments are essentially frequency-sensitive vacuum-tube voltmeters which can be used to measure the strength of harmonics of a test tone.

Test Meters

Every electronic technician needs a volt-ohm-milliammeter (VOM) for routing measurements and troubleshooting. One of the 20,000-ohm-per-volt type is preferable to one of lower resistance to avoid undue loading of high-resistance circuits. A vacuum-tube voltmeter (VTVM) is another essential tool for measuring and monitoring AVC voltage. If equipped with an RF probe (Figs. 2-17A and 2-17B), an AC VTVM can be used for measuring RF voltages at CB operating frequencies.

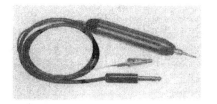

(A) Heath Model W-309-C RF probe assembly.

Courtesy Heath Co.

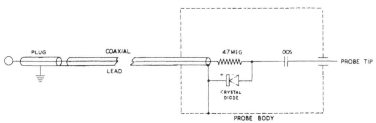

(B) Schematic diagram of RF probe.

Fig. 2-17. RF probe.

Grid-Dip Meters

A grid-dip meter is handy to have for checking out tuned circuits. A shorted turn in a coil or an open low-value capaci-

33

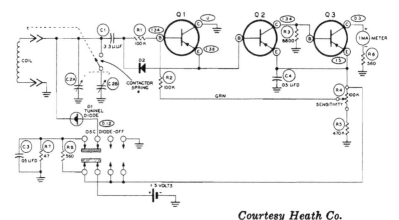

Courtesy Heath Co.

Fig. 2-18. Resonance meter.

tor may be hard to detect, except by measuring the frequency at which the tuned circuit is resonant. There are several grid-dip meters on the market which are tunable through CB range.

One of the interesting new devices of this type is not actually a grid-dip meter, but it performs the same functions. As shown in Fig. 2-18, it employs a tunnel diode as an oscillator and a transistorized meter amplifier. When its coil is placed close to the coil of a tuned circuit, and C2 is tuned to the resonant frequency of the tuned circuit being checked, the meter needle dips as in a grid dip meter. Plug-in coils provide coverage from 3 mc to 260 mc.

Oscilloscope

Since its introduction during the depression as a radio servicing instrument, the oscilloscope has been in the do-you-really-need-it category. For servicing TV sets it is essential, but many radio servicemen have chosen to ignore it, mainly because they do not understand its capabilities.

For servicing CB sets, a scope is very useful for measuring modulation. For measuring modulation using the trapezoid pattern method, as explained later, direct access to the scope tube's vertical-deflection plates is required. Some scopes are equipped with terminal boards for this purpose. For observing the RF carrier envelope, the scope vertical-amplifier channel must be able to handle frequencies in the megacycle region. As will be explained later, it is not essential for the scope to handle frequencies in the 27-mc (CB) region.

Crystal Checkers

Crystals can usually be checked by measuring receiver or transmitter performance, and by trying new crystals. An external crystal checker can be used for determining relative activity of a crystal. When using the instrument shown in Fig. 2-19, the crystal is merely plugged into the checker and

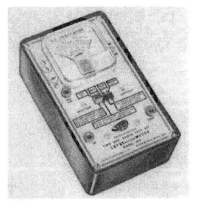

Fig. 2-19. Portable crystal checker.

Courtesy Seco Mfg. Co.

its relative activity is indicated on a meter. The crystal is operated in an oscillator circuit in the tester, which may also be used as a signal generator for receiver alignment.

Shop CB Set

A CB set is a handy shop test instrument. For this purpose the set should be one of the types that can transmit and receive on all 23 channels. The transmitter is used as a frequency reference, or signal generator, for receiver alignment. It can also be used for making quick transmitter frequency checks. The receiver can be used for making modulation measurements when used with a scope, and as part of a transmitter frequency measurement set-up. Procedures for using CB sets as test instruments are explained later.

By adding an external S-meter, available in kit or wired form, a shop CB receiver which does not have a built-in S-meter can be used as a high-sensitivity field-strength meter.

Bench Power Supply

It is essential, when servicing CB sets in a shop, to simulate actual operating conditions. In a vehicle the battery voltage can vary from 11 to 15 volts in 12-volt equipped cars, and from 5.5 to 7.5 volts in 6-volt equipped cars. Receiver sensitivity and transmitter power output vary widely with battery voltage. When voltage is high, the receiver might burst into oscillation, and transmitter power input might exceed the legal limit of 5 watts.

Since some CB sets operate from a 6-volt source, it is essential to have both 6- and 12-volt bench power supplies. Two 6-volt batteries can be used in series to get 12 volts, and 6 volts at their junction. But, batteries alone will not give you a variable voltage power source. If you float a battery charger (Fig. 2-20) across the batteries, you can vary the voltage by turning the charger on and off.

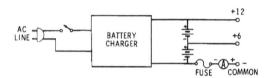

Fig. 2-20. 6/12-volt battery power supply.

An ammeter in the common power lead (Fig. 20) makes trouble diagnosis easier since you can tell immediately if input current is lower or higher than normal. A 0-15 DC ammeter, protected by a fuse, is suitable for this purpose.

Rectifier power supply—Several variable voltage-rectifier power supplies on the market can be adjusted to deliver from zero to 15 volts DC output. A typical circuit is shown in Fig.

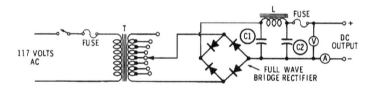

Fig. 2-21. Variable DC power supply.

2-21. The AC line voltage is stepped down by transformer T whose secondary has numerous taps selected by a switch. The low AC voltage is rectified by a full-wave bridge rectifier and filtered by L, C1, and C2. A DC voltmeter and DC ammeter provide load voltage and current indications.

Variable AC voltage source—While the nominal AC line voltage is 117 volts, it can be anywhere from 105 to 130 volts

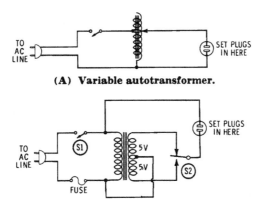

(A) Variable autotransformer.

(B) Buck-boost transformer circuit.

Fig. 2-22. Variable AC power supplies.

in some areas. If a CB set is operated at too high or too low a voltage, performance is affected. Since wide variations in line voltages are apt to be encountered by customers, it is a good idea to check out sets in the shop at the extreme limits of line voltage. To do this a variable autotransformer, such as the *Variac*, may be connected between the AC line and the set. The voltage to the set can be varied from zero to 135 volts. Fig. 2-22A is a schematic of such a device. The voltage is varied by adjustment of a knob, which varies the turns ratio of the autotransformer.

Input voltage can be stepped up or down 5 volts by employing a center-tapped 10-volt filament transformer as an autotransformer (Fig. 2-22B). When the SPDT switch is set in one position, the line voltage is boosted 5 volts (half of the secondary voltage), and when set in the other position, line voltage is dropped 5 volts.

Useful Life of Test Equipment

When buying test equipment, the investment must be justified by the monetary return that can be realized. Most test equipment can be expected to have a useful life of 10 years. Some may become obsolete more rapidly if FCC regulations or manufacturers' standards are tightened. The uses for the test equipment described so far are explained in subsequent chapters.

Chapter 3

Frequency Selection and Control

A typical CB set employs at least two oscillators for generating an RF signal. One is the transmitter oscillator, which must be crystal-controlled; the other is the receiver local oscillator, which may be crystal-controlled, fixed-tuned without crystal control, or tunable. A super-regenerative receiver is used in some CB sets. If the receiver employs a separate quench oscillator, it is generally fixed-tuned, but not crystal-controlled. Most employ a self-quenching detector which swings in and out of oscillation at a supersonic rate.

TRANSMITTER OSCILLATORS

The transmitter section of a CB set must be crystal-controlled so that it will operate within ± 0.005% of the selected operating frequency. A block diagram of a typical CB trans-

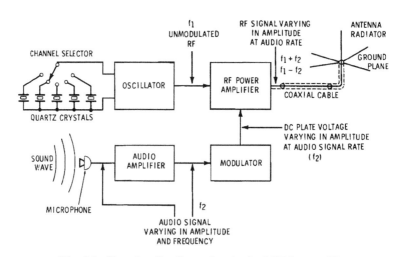

Fig. 3-1. Signal paths through a typical CB transmitter.

mitter is shown in Fig. 3-1. The oscillator operates at a frequency determined by the crystal that is in use. To change frequency of a single-channel transmitter, the crystal is replaced. In a multichannel transmitter, the channel selector is set to select the desired crystal.

The unmodulated high-frequency output of the oscillator is fed to the RF power amplifier which usually operates at the same frequency as the oscillator. The crystal may be of the third overtone type, i.e., a crystal which is ground to one-fourth of the operating frequency, but exercises frequency control at its fourth harmonic (third overtone).

When unmodulated, the RF power amplifier feeds a CW (continuous-wave) signal into the antenna system. This signal (f1) is of constant amplitude and frequency. But, when modulated, the signal being fed into the antenna varies in amplitude at audio modulating rate f2. The signal is no longer a single frequency. Instead, it consists of a carrier, at oscillator frequency f1, and two sidebands. The width of the upper and lower sidebands produced by amplitude modulation is equal to the audio modulating frequency (f2). If the highest modulating frequency is 3,000 cps, the radiated signal occupies spectrum space extending from f1–f2 to f1+f2; hence the signal, called A3 emission, occupies 6 kilocycles of the radio spectrum.

RECEIVERS

The radiated signal must be demodulated in order to use the audio signal. At a very short distance, the receiver could consist simply of a detector and audio amplifier. The signal at the input to the detector includes f1 + f2 and f1–f2. At the output of the detector f2 is amplified and then converted back into sound waves by a speaker.

A practical CB receiver block diagram is shown in Fig. 3-2. The incoming A3 signal (f1+f2 and f1–f2) is amplified and heterodyned in the mixer stage with local oscillator signal f3, which is of constant frequency and amplitude.

The output of the mixer contains many signals including f1+f2, f1–f2, f3+ (f1+f2), f3+(f1–f2), f3–(f1+f2) and f3–(f1–f2). The output of the mixer is tuned to f4, which is equal to f1–f3, or f1 + f3, depending on whether f3 is higher or lower than f1. The IF amplifier therefore passes f4+f2 and f4–f2 when receiving an AM signal.

If incoming carrier f1 is at 27.025 mc and local-oscillator signal f3 is at 26.570 mc, IF signal f4 will be at 455 kc. The

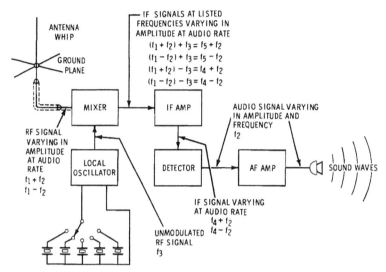

Fig. 3-2. Signal paths through a typical CB receiver.

incoming signal, when amplitude modulated at 3,000 cps, will extend from 27.022 mc to 27.028 mc (6 kc wide). When mixed with 26.570 mc local-oscillator signal f3, IF signal f4 will extend from 452 kc to 458 kc.

This double sideband AM signal, after amplification, is demodulated by the detector and only f2 remains. This signal is amplified by the audio amplifier and converted into sound by the speaker.

Fig. 3-2 shows that the local oscillator can be set to any of five frequencies by selecting the appropriate crystal. Each of these crystals operates at a frequency 455 kc below (or above) the desired receiving frequency.

FREQUENCY STABILITY

To meet FCC technical standards, the transmitter frequency must not vary more than +0.005% from the channel frequency. This means that at 27.025 mc, for example, the transmitter carrier frequency must remain within 1,351 cps of 27.052 mc, since 27.052 kc × 0.005% equals 1.351 kc or 1,351 cps (0.005% = 0.00005).

While the receiver local oscillator does not have to be crystal controlled, it is important that its frequency setting remain relatively stable. This is particularly true in highly selective receivers. If the incoming signal is at 27.025 mc and the IF

40

is 455 kc, the local oscillator is normally tuned to 26.570 mc. If the local oscillator drifts, the IF will no longer be at 455 kc. If the receiver bandwidth is narrow, distortion and reduced sensitivity will result when the local oscillator drifts excessively.

CRYSTALS

The original crystals furnished by the manufacturer of the CB set were ground specifically for use in that particular make and model. When replacement crystals are installed, or when channels are added, it is best to obtain crystals from the maker or distributor of the CB unit. When ordering crystals directly from a crystal manufacturer, or through a parts distributor, the make and model of the CB set should be specified. The frequency of a crystal oscillator is determined not only by the crystal, but also by the capacity and inductance of the associated circuitry.

Using Stock Crystals

There are available, at radio parts distributors and from mail order houses, Citizens band crystals which have been ground for use in circuits under "typical" conditions. In some sets they will operate at the labelled frequency within the legal 0.005% tolerance. In other sets, their use may result in unlawful, off-frequency operation.

Whenever installing new crystals in a customer's transmitter, always measure the frequency before turning the set over to the customer. If you don't, you may put the customer in jeopardy of being cited by the FCC for off-frequency operation.

Crystal Trimming

When a new crystal causes a transmitter to operate at a frequency that is *higher* than the intended channel frequency, proper operation can often be obtained by adding a small-value capacitor across the crystal, as shown by the dotted lines in Fig. 3-3. The capacitor may be a small variable air dielectric

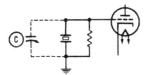

Fig. 3-3. Frequency-trimming capacitor connected across crystal.

capacitor, such as the Hammarlund MAC-5, which has a capacity range of 1.4 mmf to 5.0 mmf.

Adjust the capacitor until the transmitter is exactly on frequency, as measured with a frequency meter accurate to at least 0.0025%. Do not add a crystal-trimming capacitor unless a frequency meter is available with which to determine that operation on the correct frequency results.

The added trimmer capacitor must be installed close to the crystal, using the shortest possible leads. Its adjustment must be sealed and must not be changed, except by a licensed operator, or under his supervision.

In a multichannel transmitter the crystal-trimmer capacitor should be connected across only the crystal whose operating

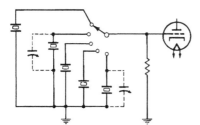

Fig. 3-4. Trimmer capacitors may be required across each channel crystal in a multichannel transmitter.

frequency is to be reduced, as shown in Fig. 3-4. In some cases, a capacitor may be required across more than one crystal.

When a new crystal operates too *low* in frequency, it may be difficult to increase the frequency since it is necessary to reduce circuit capacity, inductance, or both. It is much easier to obtain the correct crystal or add a capacitor across a crystal that operates normally at a slightly higher frequency.

Some CB transmitters are equipped with crystal trimmers at the factory to enable licensed service technicians to set the crystals exactly on frequency. The oscillator tank (LC) is compromise-tuned for equal-as-possible operation on all channels.

FREQUENCY MULTIPLIERS

Some CB transmitters employ an oscillator that operates at a lower frequency than the operating frequency. The crystal oscillator frequency is a submultiple of the operating frequency. For transmission on 27.025 mc, for example, the oscillator could operate at 6,756.25 kc. This signal is then passed through a frequency quadrupler.

42

DOUBLE-CONVERSION RECEIVERS

Double-conversion superheterodyne receiver circuits are used in some CB sets in order to achieve better selectivity. Fig. 3-5 is a block diagram of this type of receiver. Incoming HF signal f1 is heterodyned to a lower frequency (f4) by mixing it with local oscillator signal f3.

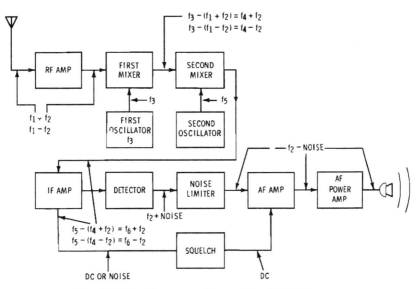

Fig. 3-5. Double-conversion receiver block diagram.

This IF signal (f4) is heterodyned down to a still lower frequency (f6) by mixing f4 with another local oscillator signal (f5). If f1 is at 27.025 mc and f3 is at 16.325 mc, f4 will be at 10.7 mc. If f4 at 10.7 mc is mixed with f5 at 10.245 mc, f6 will be at 455 kc. The resulting f6 beat signal, with its sidebands, will extend from 452 mc (f6–f2) to 458 mc (f6+f2) when an AM signal, modulated at 3,000 cps, is received.

CHANNEL SELECTION

As pointed out earlier, the transmitter frequency is determined, by the crystal used in the oscillator. The frequency at which the receiver will be most sensitive depends on the frequency of the local oscillator in a single-conversion superheterodyne receiver (Fig. 3-2). In a fixed-tuned, crystal-controlled single-channel receiver, it is necessary to change

43

the crystal when changing receiving frequency. In a multi-channel receiver the channel-selector switch is set to select the required crystal. In a tunable receiver, the oscillator can be tuned manually over a frequency range extending from 26.96 mc to 27.26 mc plus or minus the IF.

In a double-conversion superheterodyne receiver, frequency may be changed by changing the frequency of either the first or second local oscillator. This is done by changing crystals or switching in the correct crystal with the channel-selector switch. In a tunable receiver the second oscillator is generally tunable over a 290-kc range to permit selection of any of the 23 channels.

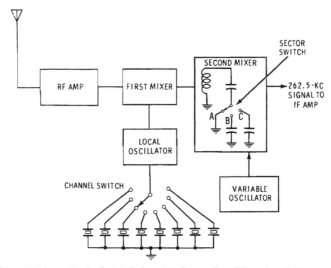

Fig. 3-6. A method of obtaining 24 channels with only eight crystals.

CRYSTAL SYNTHESIZERS

Crystal-synthesizer circuits are used in some 23-channel, fixed-tuned receivers. As shown in block diagram Fig. 3-9, only eight crystals are required to tune to any of the 23 channels. The eight crystals are ground for the consecutive frequency channels. The output of the first mixer is adjustable by the sector switch to any of three intermediate frequencies. Hence, the eight crystal frequencies can be translated into 24 frequencies, of which 23 are utilized.

In the Hammarlund CB-23, this type of frequency selection circuit is employed. In addition, the second local oscillator

44

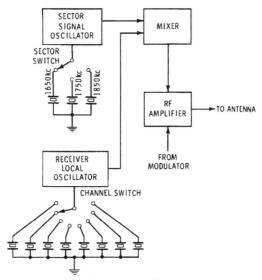

Fig. 3-7. Block diagram of Hammarlund CB-23.

is tunable ±3 kc, providing a fine tuning adjustment which does not affect transmitter frequency.

The eight receiver crystals are also used to control transmitter frequency, as shown in block diagram Fig. 3-7. The receiver crystal frequencies are heterodyned in a mixer against any of three crystal-controlled sector-oscillator frequencies. The resulting beat signals are at the 23 CB frequencies.

OSCILLATOR TROUBLES

Unstable transmitter operation often results from improper tuning of the plate circuit at the oscillator stage. In some circuits the plate-tank inductance is varied by adjustment of its core; and in some transmitters this inductance may be of a fixed value, and the plate-tank capacitor may be adjustable.

When tuning the oscillator plate circuit, the results may be noted by observing changes in transmitter output or by monitoring the DC bias voltage at the grid of the RF amplifier with a DC vacuum-tube voltmeter connected through a high-value, series, isolating resistor. The isolating resistor should be at the end of the lead so that the meter lead will not detune the circuit.

Initially, tune the variable plate-tank component for maximum meter reading (resonance). Presence of voltage indicates that the oscillator is functioning, since the bias voltage exists

45

only when an RF signal from the oscillator is present. The RF signal, when swinging positive, is partially shorted out by the rectifier action of the grid and cathode. But, when swinging negative, the grid looks like an open circuit. Thus, a negative DC voltage appears across the grid-leak resistor and is sustained by the coupling capacitor.

After tuning the variable plate-tank component for maximum meter reading, adjust it in one direction and then the other and note that the meter reading falls off faster in one direction than the other. Now, adjust the plate tank to a point on the more gentle slope side of the maximum meter reading. This point should be below maximum, but as high as possible without loss of stability. Key the transmitter on and off when these adjustments are made until a point is reached where the meter reading appears and stays constant each time the transmitter is turned on. If set too close to maximum, the oscillator may fail to start. In a multichannel transmitter, adjustment of the plate tank must be a compromise for all channels.

Defective Crystals

Unstable oscillator operation or insufficient oscillator output, as indicated by low-bias readings, can be due to low crystal activity. Try a new crystal, even of another frequency, and note if there is any increase in bias voltage. If a new crystal shows marked improvement, install a new crystal of appropriate frequency. Whenever installing a new crystal, measure the transmitter frequency.

Insufficient Oscillator Output

If the oscillator output is too low, there will not be enough RF amplifier drive to secure maximum transmitter power output. Low oscillator output may be caused by a weak crystal, poor oscillator tube or change in value of the oscillator grid-leak resistor.

RECEIVER FREQUENCY CALIBRATION

A tunable CB receiver should be capable of receiving on any frequency between 26.96 and 27.26 mc. In a single-conversion superheterodyne receiver, the local oscillator is tunable over a range of 300 kc, displaced above or below the receiving frequency by an amount determined by the intermediate frequency of the receiver. For example, if the IF is

1,650 kc, the oscillator should be tunable through the 25.31-25.61-mc range or 28.61-28.91-mc range (usually the former).

Single-Conversion Receivers

A tunable single-conversion superhet can be easily calibrated; merely set your frequency meter to 27.255 mc (channel 23) and set the receiver tuning dial to channel 23, with the frequency meter pick-up lead near the receiver antenna terminal. Monitor receiver AVC voltage with a VTVM, and adjust the receiver tuning dial for maximum meter reading. If maximum reading is not obtained at the channel-23 point on the receiver tuning dial, adjust the receiver oscillator trimmer until maximum meter reading is obtained.

Now set the receiver tuning dial to channel 1 and the frequency meter to 26.965 mc. Maximum AVC voltage should be obtained with the receiver tuning dial set exactly to chan-

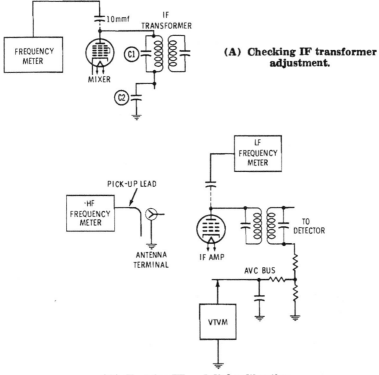

(A) Checking IF transformer adjustment.

(B) Test for IF and dial calibration.

Fig. 3-8. Measuring IF amplifier tuning.

nel 1. Check out several (or all) channels in the same manner. If the receiver tuning dial does not track, adjust the oscillator trimmer for optimum tracking through its scale.

Measuring IF—If the dial calibration is sufficiently inaccurate, it may be necessary to replace oscillator components which have changed in value. Or, the receiver IF may not be tuned to the correct frequency. This can be checked out as shown in Fig. 3-8A. If you have a tunable frequency meter (such as a BC-221) that covers the IF range, connect its pickup lead through a 10-mmf capacitor to the plate of the mixer tube. Monitor AVC voltage and tune the frequency meter for maximum meter reading. If the frequency meter indicates that the IF is not at the correct frequency, retune the IF transformers for maximum AVC voltage with the frequency meter set at the correct IF.

Then connect the LF frequency meter to the last IF amplifier, as shown in Fig. 3-8B. Set an HF frequency meter to any CB channel (loosely coupled to receiver input) and adjust the receiver tuning dial to the selected channel. You should hear an audio beat note as you tune the receiver past the selected channel setting since the LF frequency meter signal beats against the IF signal. If the receiver dial is correctly calibrated, zero beat should occur at the selected channel dial setting.

Measuring oscillator frequency—The calibration of the tuning dial can also be checked by loosely coupling a continuously tunable HF frequency meter (input terminal) to the plate of the receiver mixer tube, as shown in Fig. 3-8A, and measuring the actual oscillator frequency. This permits tapping the oscillator signal without detuning the oscillator as might occur if the connection were made directly to the oscillator. When no external radio signal is being recieved, only the oscillator signal is present at the plate of the mixer. It is partially shorted to ground through C1 and C2. Another way to tap the oscillator signal is to drape the signal generator pick-up lead near the oscillator coil.

Set the frequency meter to the frequency equal to 27.255 mc minus (or plus) the receiver IF, e.g., 27.255–1.650 = 25.605 mc. Adjust the receiver dial until the frequency meter indicates that the known frequency (frequency meter) and unknown frequency (receiver oscillator) are the same. The receiver tuning dial should be at the channel-23 setting. Repeat for channel 1 and various intermediate channels. Adjust the oscillator trimmer as required.

Quick calibration check—If you have a 23-channel CB set available, which is known to be *on frequency*, dial-calibration checks can be made more quickly. Connect the 23-channel shop test set and the set being serviced to individual dummy antenna loads with a VTVM to the AVC bus of the set being serviced. Set the shop set to each channel, 1 through 23, turning the transmitter on momentarily at each channel setting. Tune the receiver being serviced to each channel for maximum AVC voltage, noting dial-calibration accuracy.

Dual-Conversion Receivers

In a dual-conversion superhet, either the first local oscillator or the second is tunable. If the first local oscillator is tunable, the procedures just described are applicable, except the IF measurement should be made at the grid or plate of the second mixer. When the second local oscillator is tunable, the first local oscillator is generally crystal controlled. Its frequency can be measured by using the setup shown in Fig. 3-8A, or loosely coupling an HF frequency meter to the first oscillator. The frequency meter is tuned to zero beat with the first local ōscillator (if the frequency meter is of the continuous tuning type) and the frequency is determined from the calibration chart. If the crystal operates at more than 1 kc from its marked frequency, try a new one.

When using a difference-type frequency meter, which is not equipped with a crystal for the nonstandard first-oscillator frequency, set the frequency meter to one of the CB channels and couple it loosely to the receiver input. Monitor AVC voltage and tune the receiver dial for maximum meter reading. The receiver-dial channel setting and frequency-meter setting should coincide.

If they do not, trim the second oscillator at channel 23, using the frequency meter as the signal source, until the tuning dial reading is correct. Check the calibration accuracy at channel 1 and several intermediate channels. If the dial does not track correctly, try a new first-oscillator crystal, look for changes in second oscillator components, or measure the low IF.

The low IF can be measured with a continuously tunable LF frequency meter by connecting it to the plate of the second mixer (Fig. 3-8A) and tuning it for maximum AVC voltage, as described earlier. If a difference-type frequency meter equipped with an appropriate IF crystal is used, inject the signal in the same manner and tune the IF as above.

When using a 23-channel CB set as a reference-signal generator, the difference-type frequency meter (set to receiver low IF) can be coupled to the last IF stage, as shown in Fig. 3-8B. When an RF signal is being received from the shop CB test set, the low IF signal generated in the receiver can be read directly by the frequency meter. It should be within 1 kc of the correct IF. The receiver IF signal will only be at the correct frequency when the incoming signal and both local oscillators are at their correct frequencies.

Fixed-Tuned Receivers

The frequencies of receiver crystals can be measured with a continuously tunable HF frequency meter by using the setup shown in Fig. 3-8A. At each channel setting, measure the frequency. If any crystal is off much more than 1 kc from its marked frequency, it should be replaced.

A quicker way is to use a 23-channel CB set as a signal generator. Couple a continuously tunable LF frequency meter (such as BC-221) to the IF amplifier, as shown in Fig. 3-8B. With both sets switched to the same channel and the shop set transmitting, tune the frequency meter for zero beat in the receiver speaker, or in the frequency-meter speaker or headphones. Compare the frequency-meter reading with the rated receiver IF. Repeat for all channels.

When using a difference-type frequency meter equipped with an appropriate IF crystal, variations in receiver IF can be read directly in terms of deviation from standard. The ear can also be used to detect the approximate frequency of the resulting beat note heard in the speaker. The beat note should be less than approximately 1,000 cps at each channel setting.

If the measured IF differs widely from channel to channel (it will differ to some extent due to crystal tolerances in both sets), it is an indication that the receiver crystals are not correctly matched.

In a dual-conversion, fixed-tuned receiver one of the local oscillators is generally operated at a single frequency and the other is switched. It is important that the single-frequency oscillator be at the correct frequency since it affects all channels.

TRANSMITTER-FREQUENCY MEASUREMENT

For maximum ease and accuracy, a difference-type frequency meter equipped with crystals for all 23 CB channels is recommended. Connect a dummy antenna load to the transmitter and place the frequency meter near the transmitter. The transmitter signal is picked-up by a short piece of wire or a plug-in antenna connected to the frequency meter. Sometimes the frequency meter is connected directly to the transmitter through coaxial jumper cables and an attenuator. In this matter, your frequency meter instruction book should be consulted.

Set the frequency meter and the transmitter to the channel to be measured. Allow the CB set to warm up (receiver on, transmitter off). Turn the transmitter on and read the deviation in frequency from the correct value directly on the meter. Modulate the transmitter briefly to see if the frequency changes—it should not. Repeat this process for each channel to be checked. If any one is off more than 500 cps (0.5 kc), replace the appropriate transmitter crystal, or adjust the crystal padder, if there is one, for zero deviation from the correct frequency.

While the FCC tolerance for CB transmitters is 0.005%, or approximately 1,300 cps, you must allow for error in the frequency meter. If your frequency meter is accurate to 0.0025%, make 500 cps difference in known and unknown frequencies your standard. However, if your frequency meter is accurate to 0.00025,% as some are, you can lower your standard to 1,000 cps.

Using Heterodyne Frequency Meters

You can use a surplus BC-221 frequency meter for many purposes, but it is not suitable by itself for measuring CB transmitter frequencies, except on a secondary basis. Its basic design has been utilized in more modern, more accurate heterodyne-type frequency meters which are suitable for CB frequency measurements. They are not as easy to use as difference-type frequency meters, but they are more flexible.

Connect a dummy antenna load to the transmitter being checked. Allow the set to warm up (transmitter off, receiver on). Check the calibration and allow the frequency meter to warm up as specified in its instruction book. Tune the frequency meter to the frequency to be measured, as noted in a chart or calibration curve. Turn the transmitter on and adjust the frequency meter for zero beat, as heard in its speaker or headphones (some instruments are more complex).

Note the frequency-meter dial reading and read the measured frequency from the calibration curve. That is all there

51

is to it; but watch out for errors in reading the dial and the calibration curve.

If the CB transmitter has crystal padders, set the frequency meter to the desired frequency and adjust the padder for zero beat. Do this for every channel for which the transmitter is equipped.

Quick frequency check—Relative transmitter frequency can be checked quickly with a calibrated, fixed-tuned, multichannel CB receiver and a calibrated IF signal source. The CB receiver and the IF signal source form a heterodyne frequency meter. If the receiver is of the 23-channel type, the setup shown in Fig. 3-9 can be used to check transmitters operating on any of the CB channels.

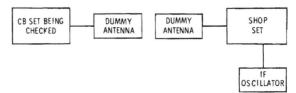

Fig. 3-9. Quick frequency check setup.

SHOP-RECEIVER CALIBRATION

The receiver of the Hammarlund CB-23 is ideal for this purpose. It has a fine-tuning knob which should be removed and replaced with a dial having a scale. Inject a signal into the last IF amplifier from an LF frequency meter (such as BC-221) set to 262.5 kc (Fig. 3-8B). Apply a signal from a calibrated frequency meter at each CB channel frequency into the receiver input, working through from channel 1 to 23. Adjust the fine-tuning dial for zero beat as heard in the shop receiver speaker. Record the dial reading. This is the *channel reference point*. Then set the LF frequency meter to 262.0 kc and adjust the fine-tuning dial for zero beat and record the dial reading. This is the *low-frequency-limit* reference point. Now set the LF frequency meter to 263.0 kc and again adjust the fine-tuning dial for zero beat. Record the dial reading, which is the *high-frequency-limit reference point*. Repeat this process for all 23 channels making three frequency-reference points for each channel, −0.5 kc, on-frequency, and +0.5 kc.

Quick-Check Procedure

To measure the frequency of a transmitter, connect dummy antenna loads to the shop receiver and to the transmitter being serviced, as shown in Fig. 3-9, and set both CB units to the same channel. Set the shop unit fine-tuning dial to the *channel reference point* mentioned in the preceding paragraph.

Set the LF frequency meter to 262.5 kc (or use a 262.5 kc crystal-controlled oscillator instead of the tunable LF frequency meter). Turn on the transmitter and adjust the shop receiver fine-tuning dial for zero beat, as heard in the receiver speaker. From your record determine whether zero beat occurs between the +0.5-kc-limit reference points for the channel being checked.

Adjustable LF Reference Signal

The receiver of a 23-channel CB set which does not have a fine-tuning adjustment can also be used for quick check of transmitter frequencies. Inject a signal at the receiver low IF into the last IF amplifier (Fig. 3-8B) and a signal from an HF frequency meter at each of the CB channel frequencies into the receiver input, working through from channel 1 through 23. Tune the LF frequency meter at each channel for zero beat as heard in the receiver speaker and note and record the frequency to which the frequency meter is set.

To measure the frequency of a transmitter, connect the equipment as shown in Fig. 3-9. Turn the transmitter on, with the test receiver set to the same channel, and tune the LF frequency meter for zero beat. Note the frequency meter reading and compare it with the correct reading for that channel. If there is a difference of more than 0.5 kc, you can assume that the transmitter is off frequency.

The preceding frequency-measuring techniques are satisfactory for quick checking and are not a substitute for precise measurement with an HF frequency meter. When the shop frequency meter is being used elsewhere, a calibrated shop receiver and an LF frequency meter (such as the inexpensive BC-221) will give you a quick means for determining transmitter frequencies.

MEASURING FREQUENCY OF DISTANT STATIONS

The quick-check techniques can be used to measure frequencies of on-the-air signals by connecting the shop receiver to an antenna.

Or, you can use a shop receiver and an HF frequency meter, loosely coupled to the receiver input, to determine the frequency of an on-the-air signal. If of the continuously tun-

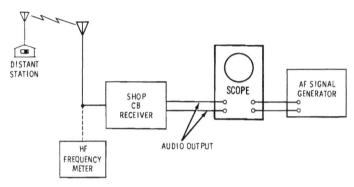

Fig. 3-10. Checking transmitted signal frequency.

able type, the frequency meter is tuned to zero beat with the on-the-air signal and the frequency meter reading noted. When a crystal-controlled frequency meter (difference-type) is used, the frequency of the resulting audio beat note can be measured with an oscilloscope and audio signal generator (Fig. 3-10). The audio signal generator is tuned to the same frequency, as indicated by a 1:1 pattern on the scope screen. The frequency indicated by the audio signal generator is equal to the difference between the two signals (it should be less than 500 cps).

FCC REQUIREMENTS

CB transmitter frequencies are measured for two purposes, to secure maximum performance and to determine if FCC regulations are being violated. When measuring transmitter frequencies, record the information obtained in case the FCC wants to know when and how the measurements were made, and what the results were. In these records, "OK" is meaningless. Spell out the frequency as measured, exactly in megacycles, kilocycles, and cycles per second.

Although the FCC does not currently require CB licenses to have transmitter frequencies checked at regular intervals, they can demand that frequencies be checked, and they *can* take other action, when off-frequency operation occurs.

The quick-check frequency-measuring techniques described here are not satisfactory for FCC record purposes since there are too many variables. A calibrated HF frequency meter of known accuracy must be used for FCC purposes. A meter designed especially for CB servicing is shown in figure 3-11.

Fig. 3-11. Frequency meter for measurements in 25-50 mc range.

Calibrating Frequency Meters

A frequency meter should be calibrated at regular intervals. A precise secondary frequency standard or electronic counter can be used for this purpose, but such equipment is expensive and seldom found in a service establishment. A frequency meter should be sent back to the manufacturer, or to an instrument service center recommended by the manufacturer for periodic calibration.

55

Chapter 4

Power Amplifiers and Modulators

The transmitter oscillator is always followed by one or more RF amplifier stages since direct modulation of the oscillator can affect the oscillator frequency stability. Generally, the oscillator tank and power amplifier are tuned to the same frequency, except when a frequency multiplier or a crystal synthesizer circuit (Fig. 3-6) is used.

Transmitter-functioning tests and adjustments should always be made with the CB-set antenna connector terminated into a dummy-load antenna, either directly, through a through-line-type RF power meter, or directly into an RF power meter which contains a dummy load. Transmitter performance can be measured and monitored by metering power-amplifier grid drive (DC bias on grid), power-amplifier plate or cathode current, and/or relative RF power output. Power input to the final RF stage of the transmitter is determined by measuring the plate voltage and plate current and then multiplying the voltage times the current (in amperes). The answer is the power input in watts. In a transistorized unit, collector current is measured. Some transmitters are provided with test points for making these measurements. The procedures in the service manual should be followed.

With 5-watts input, the output, as measured with an RF power meter, may range from 1 to 3.5 watts, depending on the efficiency of the transmitter.

POWER-AMPLIFIER TROUBLES

The most common trouble in the RF power-amplifier or buffer or frequency-multiplier stage is a defective tube. The quickest method to find out whether or not you have tube trouble is to try a new tube. When a new tube is installed, retune the circuit to offset any differences in the interelectrode capacities of the tubes. A common symptom of tube trouble

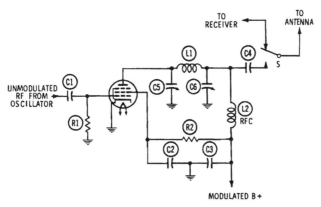

Fig. 4-1. RF power amplifier using pi-network.

is lower-than-normal power output or rapid fall-off of power after turning on the transmitter.

A typical RF power-amplifier circuit is shown in Fig. 4-1. A pi-network is used in the plate circuit. Improper operation can be the result of a significant change in the value of grid-leak resistor R1. Low transmitter output can be caused by low screen voltage due to leakage through C2 or an increase in the value of R2. If C2 is open, the RF amplifier may oscillate and cause unlawful emission. If C3 is open, RF energy can reach the modulator and cause distortion; if C3 is shorted, the transmitter will not operate; and if C3 is leaky, power output will be reduced. Capacitor C4, if open, will reduce or cut off transmitter output. If shorted, C4 will apply dangerous high voltage to the antenna.

If L2 is open, there will be no voltage at the RF-amplifier plate; and if L1 has a shorted turn, it may absorb RF energy and reduce transmitter power. Obviously, if L1 is open or has a shorted turn, the plate-tank circuit cannot be tuned to proper resonance by adjustment of C5 and C6. Accumulation of dirt across the insulation or the plates of C5 and C6 can cause power loss due to leakage and low circuit Q. Wipe off dirt and gently blow out dust that may have accumulated on the plates.

Another source of trouble is at the antenna relay or switch (S) contacts. These contacts must be clean, and they must close firmly—never file or sandpaper these contacts. Clean them with a suitable chemical or burnishing tool. Better yet, replace the relay or switch with a new one if contact trouble is experienced.

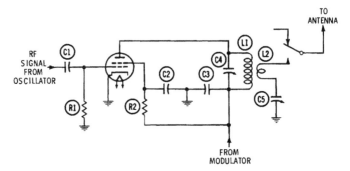

Fig. 4-2. A commonly used parallel resonant plate circuit.

Unstable RF-amplifier operation, such as the tendency to self-oscillate, indicates changes in component values, excessive voltages, improper lead dress, and, in some cases, improper design. Some transmitters employ a neutralizing capacitor which must be adjusted in strict accordance with the set service manual. Whether or not a neutralizing capacitor is used, no transmitter output should be present (as noted on the RF power meter connected to the antenna terminal) when the crystal or oscillator tube is out of its socket.

Many transmitters employ the circuit shown in Fig. 4-2. The parallel, resonant plate-tank circuit (L1-C4) is inductively coupled to L2. Capacitor C5 adjusts output to the antenna. In some sets L1 is tunable. Defects in tuned-circuit components L1, L2, C4, and C5), such as leakage, can cause improper tuning and low output power due to loss of circuit Q. Open bypass capacitors (C2 and C3) can cause self-oscillation and instability.

In some sets the RF-amplifier tank is also used as the tuned circuit for the receiver RF amplifier or mixer, as shown in Fig. 4-3, so that trouble in the tank circuit may result in both receiver and transmit failures.

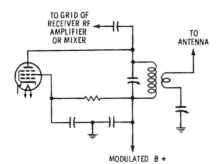

Fig. 4-3. Typical RF tank for transmitting and receiving.

58

ANTENNA SWITCHING

A switch or relay is commonly used to transfer the center conductor of the antenna transmission line from the receiver input to the transmitter output (Figs. 4-1 and 4-2). This switch or relay generally has other contacts which cut off the speaker, disable the receiver, and activate the transmitter when transmitting. In some sets (Fig. 4-3) the antenna is connected to the transmitter and receiver at all times; it is not switched.

TRANSMITTER TUNING

The same general principles apply to tuning of all CB transmitters; however, the tuning procedures outlined in the applicable instruction book (if one is available) should be followed.

If the transmitter does not have readily accessible test points for measuring power-amplifier grid drive and power-amplifier plate or cathode current, the transmitter can usually be tuned by connecting it to an RF power meter and dummy load. Tune the oscillator-tank circuit, power-amplifier tank circuit, and antenna circuit for maximum RF power output. Then back off the oscillator tuning on the gentle slope side (output drops off), as explained in Chapter 3. Alternately, retrim the power-amplifier tank circuit and antenna circuit for maximum power output.

Key the transmitter on and off; if the output is zero at any time that the transmitter is turned on, try retuning the oscillator-tank circuit. If the power output drops off after turning on the transmitter, try new tubes. Make these tests without modulation. When talking into the microphone, transmitter power output should rise.

HARMONIC FILTERS

The circuits shown so far do not have the harmonic filters that are incorporated in some transmitters. When harmonic filters are not used, interference may be caused to nearby TV receivers and other radio services. The second harmonic of some CB transmitter channels falls squarely into one of the VHF TV channels. The fifth harmonic may interfere with aviation communications and navigation devices. The sixth harmonic falls into the 152-174-mc mobile-communications band.

A wave trap is used in some CB sets to suppress second harmonic radiation. A series-resonant wave trap, shunted across the transmitter output, is shown in Fig. 4-4A. When

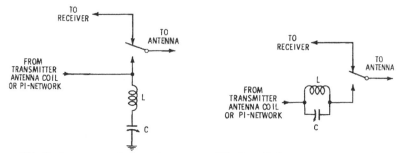

(A) Series-resonant wave trap.   (B) Parallel-resonance wave trap.

Fig. 4-4. Wave traps.

tuned to around 54.45 mc, it bypasses the second harmonics to ground, but has little effect on the transmitted signal in the 27-mc band since it has a high impedance at 27 mc.

A parallel-resonant wave trap is shown in Fig. 4-4B. When tuned to about 54.45 mc, it presents a very high impedance to passage of second harmonics. However, the desired 27-mc signal passes easily through the capacitor to the antenna. Wave traps of this type can be added to sets that do not have harmonic filters. Using a resonance chart, simply pick a coil and capacitor which can be tuned to resonance at any point between 53 and 55 mc.

To tune the wave trap, pick up the second-harmonic signal (from the transmitter) with a communications receiver tunable up to 55 mc and adjust the wave trap for minimum S meter indication. Or, set a TV set to channel 2 and adjust the wave trap until minimum TV interference is noted. Or, use a grid-dip meter to determine when the wave trap is resonant at about 54.4 mc.

More sophisticated harmonic filters are incorporated in some CB transmitters. They consist of a low pass filter which passes

Fig. 4-5. External harmonic filter.

Courtesy Gavin Instruments, Inc.

60

frequencies below 30 mc and suppresses higher frequencies. External harmonic filters, such as the one shown in Fig. 4-5, can be inserted in the coax line between the set and antenna to suppress radiation of unwanted harmonics. Such a filter is worth trying if the customer's CB transmitter is causing interference to neighboring TV receivers.

MODULATORS

All currently available CB transmitters employ AM, utilizing plate or plate-screen modulation. The basic Heising modulator is used in many CB sets. The primary of the receiver audio-output transformer is used as the modulation reactor during transmission. Plate current to both the modulator tube (which also functions as the receiver AF power amplifier) and the plate and screen of the RF power amplifier flows through the modulation reactor.

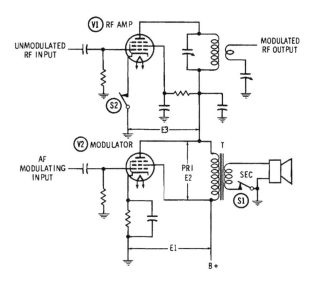

Fig. 4-6. Heising modulator.

The circuit shown in Fig. 4-6 is typical. When transmitting, switch S1 is open to avoid the effect of speaker load on the reactance of the primary of output transformer T. Current through the primary is steady when the transmitter is on (S2 closed) and there is no modulation. The RF current leaking past the plate tank is by-passed to ground through C1 and C2. Voltage E3 across the RF amplifier is equal to E1 (source voltage) minus the small DC drop, E2, across the transformer primary.

When an audio signal is fed into V2, its plate current, flowing through the transformer primary, rises and falls with the audio signal. The large audio voltage (E2) developed across the transformer primary is alternately added to or subtracted from voltage E3 that reaches the plate of V1 (E3 = E1 + E2, when E2 is of the proper polarity, and E3 = E1 - E2, when E2 is of opposing polarity).

The RF power output of the RF amplifier thus rises and falls with modulation. When fully modulated, the RF output rises 50% above the unmodulated carrier level. However, with this kind of circuit, 100% modulation is not quite reached. The circuit is popular because overmodulation is inherently prevented.

Some CB transmitters employ a special transformer, having the equivalent of three windings for achieving higher modulation percentage. The primary is tapped to form two windings connected in series-aiding (autotransformer) fashion, as shown in Fig. 4-7. The audio signal (E2A) developed across one section of the primary induces voltage E2B in the other section of the primary. These two series-aiding voltages (E2) add to or subtract from source voltage E1, causing the RF-amplifier plate and screen voltages to vary from values near zero to nearly twice E1. The entire modulator system must, of course, be designed to prevent overmodulation.

The modulator system includes a microphone, one or two stages of audio amplification, and the modulator tube and

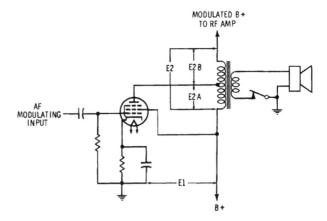

Fig. 4-7. High level modulator.

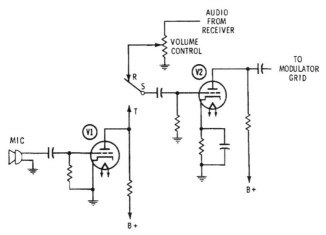

Fig. 4-8. Typical CB-transmitter speech amplifier.

reactor. Typical is the simplified circuit shown in Fig. 4-8. When receiving, only V2 is used. When transmitting, the input of V2 is switched from the receiver volume control to the output of microphone preamplifier V1.

MICROPHONE CIRCUITS

High-impedance ceramic, dynamic, and crystal microphones are commonly used with CB sets; some are used with low-impedance carbon microphones. Sometimes the receiver speaker is used as a microphone when transmitting. More audio gain is required when using one of the preceding types of high-impedance microphones than when using a carbon microphone which has much greater output. A carbon microphone requires a DC excitation voltage, whereas the other types do not.

In some sets the microphone cord is wired directly to the circuit; while in others, the microphone cord is equipped with a plug which is inserted in a microphone jack. The push-to-talk, transmit-receive control switch may be either in the microphone or on the set chassis.

High-Impedance Inputs

Microphone and modulator circuits are designed to attenuate audio frequencies above 3,000 cps, as required by the FCC. Capacitor C1 in Fig. 4-9, shunted across the high input impedance of the microphone preamplifier, increasingly at-

63

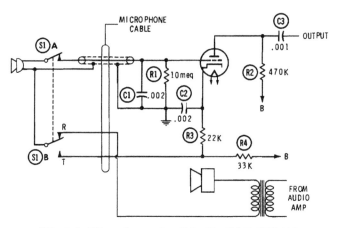

Fig. 4-9. Microphone circuit in Heathkit GW-11A.

tenuates audio frequencies as they become higher. Cathode bypass capacitor C2 is deliberately small in value so that low frequencies (below 300 cps) will be attenuated by degenerative feedback.

Releasing the press-to-talk switch inside the microphone case connects the speaker to the output transformer through the normally closed contact of S1B. The cathode of the preamplifier tube is disabled by maintaining its cathode at a relatively high positive potential (the grid is negative with respect to cathode).

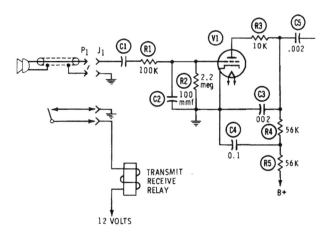

Fig. 4-10. Microphone circuit in Lafayette HE-20-C.

64

When the press-to-talk switch is operated, S1A connects the microphone to the grid of the tube. The speaker circuit is opened by S1B, which also grounds the bottom of R3 to remove the positive bias from cathode resistor R3, allowing the preamplifier to function. The shield around the microphone output lead serves as the common conductor for the transmit-receive control switch.

A fairly complex frequency-response compensation circuit is utilized in the Lafayette HE-20-C (Fig. 4-10). The microphone is connected to the grid of V1 through plug P1, jack J1, capacitor C1, and resistor R1. Together with shunt capacitor C2 and grid resistor R2, C1 and R1 form an RC filter. The output of the microphone preamplifier tube is also treated to adjust frequency response. R3 and C3 form a high-frequency attenuation circuit, and C4, because of its relatively low value, serves as a low-frequency attenuator in conjunction with R4 and R5. Depressing the switch in the microphone case energizes the transmit-receive relay, the contacts of which are not shown.

A similar input filter is shown in Fig. 4-11. A low-frequency attenuation circuit, consisting of C3 and R3, is used in the tube output circuit. Capacitor C4, shunted from plate to ground, rounds off high-frequency response. The ceramic microphone is connected at all times. The press-to-talk switch keeps the speaker connected when released, and energizes the

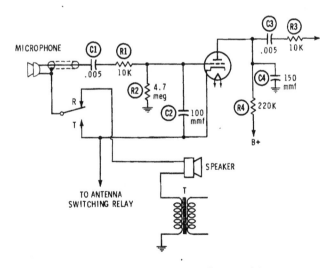

Fig. 4-11. Microphone circuit of Johnson Messenger.

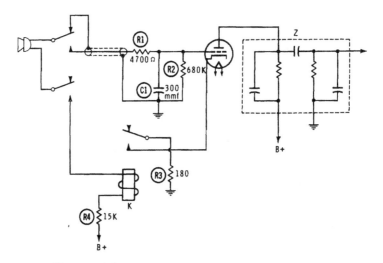

Fig. 4-12. Microphone circuit of Hammarlund CB-23.

antenna relay when pressed. Other transmit-receive wiring is not shown.

The DPDT press-to-talk switch inside the case of the ceramic microphone furnished with the Hammarlund CB-23 (Fig. 4-12) grounds the microphone when released. When depressed, the microphone is connected to the grid of the preamplifier through R1. The other section of the switch energizes transmit-receive relay K, of whose contact sets only one is shown. Capacitor C1 serves as a high-frequency input attenuator; the lack of a bypass capacitor across cathode resistor R3 reduces low-frequency response. The output of the tube is coupled to the modulator through packaged AF coupler-filter Z.

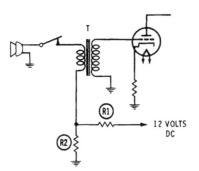

Fig. 4-13. Basic carbon-microphone circuit.

Low-Impedance Inputs

A carbon microphone is a low-impedance device (20-50 ohms) which requires a DC excitation voltage. A basic carbon-microphone input circuit is shown in Fig. 4-13. The microphone is coupled to the tube through step-up transformer T. Microphone excitation voltage is obtained at the junction of voltage divider R1-R2 from the 12-volt DC power source. The transformer steps up the voltage and the impedance.

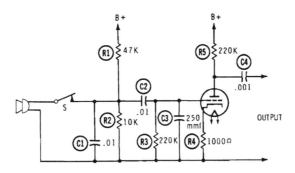

Fig. 4-14. Modified carbon-microphone circuit.

A more ingenious scheme is shown in Fig. 4-14. The microphone output is capacitively coupled to the tube. When press-to-talk switch S is closed, DC flows through the microphone. This DC is derived from the transmitter plate-voltage source at the junction of voltage divider R1-R2. The variations in current through R2, caused by sound waves acting on the microphone, are fed as an AC voltage through C2 to the grid of the tube. Capacitors C1 and C3 serve as high-frequency attenuators. Low-frequency attenuation is achieved by making C4 low in value and by not bypassing cathode resistor R4.

In the Kaar TR237B, microphone excitation voltage is obtained from the cathode of the modulator tube, as shown in Fig. 4-15. E1, the DC voltage drop due to modulator tube V2 cathode current flowing through R1 and R2, is approximately 13 volts. The audio that would otherwise appear across R1-R2 is bypassed to ground by C1. A portion of this voltage (E2), developed across R2 causes current to flow through the microphone when the press-to-talk switch is operated.

The resulting audio signal is developed across R2 and is fed to the grid through receiver volume control R3, whose setting has practically no effect on modulation level. High-frequency attenuation is provided by C2, C3, C4, C5, and C6. Low fre-

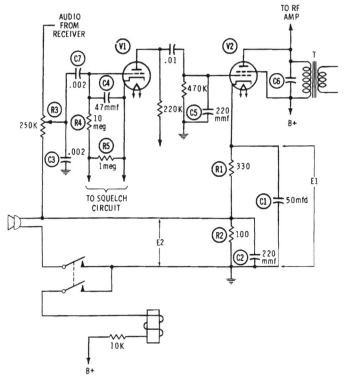

Fig. 4-15. Kaar TR237B modulator.

quencies are attenuated by C7 and the characteristics of modulation reactor/output transformer T. Tube V1 is controlled by the receiver squelch circuit (not shown), which is disabled when transmitting.

Alternate Microphone Arrangements

The microphone input circuits of CB sets must necessarily be designed to match the characteristics of the microphone furnished, or recommended for use with the set. Frequency compensation networks designed for one type of microphone may not be satisfactory for other types. For example, when a crystal microphone is fed into an input circuit of less than several megohms impedance, high-frequency response is enhanced and low frequencies are attenuated. Using an excessively long microphone cable with a crystal microphone can, on the other hand, cause excessive loss of high frequencies.

68

However, there are cases where performance can be improved by using a microphone other than that supplied with the set. Generally, high-impedance dynamic, reluctance, ceramic, and crystal microphones are interchangeable. When trying a new type of microphone, make sure that it does not overdrive the modulator and cause distortion. Also, the frequency response of a microphone can be affected by the input resistor (R1 in Fig. 4-9, for example) and a loss in effective voice power can occur.

If a new microphone causes improved transmission of high frequencies, generally resulting in more penetrating speech, it may be necessary to add high-frequency attenuation to roll off transmission of audio above 3,000 cps. This can be done by adding shunt capacity across the microphone preamplifier grid or plate. An LC filter, designed to pass voice signals below 3,000 cps, can be added ahead or behind the microphone preamplifier. The filter must, of course, have the proper input and output impedances.

A dynamic microphone can be used with a set designed for use with a carbon microphone by adding a preamplifier. The Outercom (Hammarlund) No. P26681-2 microphone contains a dynamic microphone cartridge, a single-stage transistor amplifier, and a DPST press-to-talk switch; it is equipped with a coil cord and a four-prong plug. Fig. 4-16 is a schematic diagram of the microphone assembly. Power for operation of the amplifier is derived from the transmitter plate-voltage supply as shown in the diagram. When using a microphone of this type, it is necessary to rewire the audio input circuit of the transmitter to that shown.

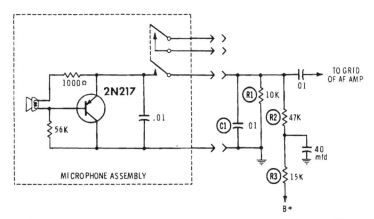

Fig. 4-16. Dynamic microphone with built-in transistor amplifier.

Handsets

Telephone-type handsets can be used with CB sets in lieu of a microphone. Handsets are available with carbon or dynamic transmitters. They are available at some radio parts jobbers, but must usually be purchased directly from the manufacturer, or a telephone-equipment distributor such as Graybar Electric Company. Handset manufacturers include General Dynamics/Telecommunications (Stromberg-Carlson), Automatic Electric Company, Kellogg, and Roanwell.

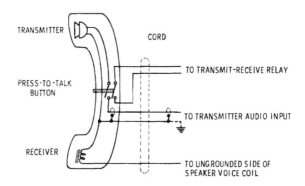

Fig. 4-17. Typical handset circuit.

A handset can be connected to a CB set, as shown in Fig. 4-17. A variable series resistance can be inserted in the audio-output lead for varying volume level. If equipped with a dynamic transmitter cartridge, a cord should be used which has a shielded conductor. When a high-output carbon transmitter cartridge is employed, a shielded lead may not be required. A regular telephone handset does not ordinarily come equipped with a cord containing a shielded conductor. Various kinds of cords are available from which a suitable type can be selected for a specific application.

MICROPHONE TROUBLES

Since a microphone is relatively inexpensive to replace, often greater customer satisfaction can be assured by selling the customer a new microphone than by attempting to repair a defective one. Microphone repairs are best made by specialists. While test devices can be rigged up for testing microphones, the cost is seldom worth the trouble. It is much easier to try a microphone and note the difference.

Defective cords and improper connections are the most common causes of microphone trouble. Some cords become stiff in cold weather and insulation may be damaged. Extreme care should be exercised when replacing or installing microphone plugs and cords to avoid cold solder joints and shorting by strands of the shield braid. Excessive *skinning-back* of the shield braid can cause annoying hum pickup. Microphone elements can become less efficient due to temperature changes, dust, and moisture. Press-to-talk switch contacts are also subject to contamination, wear, and fatigue.

Although a carbon microphone can be checked for continuity with an ohmmeter, it is better not to make this test with other types of microphones because of the danger of damaging the delicate cartridge. Some microphones will indicate an open circuit if checked with an ohmmeter.

MODULATION-SYSTEM TROUBLES

Effective communicating range is drastically reduced if modulation level is too low. If the transmitter is capable of overmodulation, its use is unlawful when modulated more than 100%, since it can cause harmful interference to others.

Low modulation is a very common trouble, resulting from improper tuning of the RF portion of the transmitter, or a defect in the modulation system. The human voice can be used as a signal source to check modulators, but it is a signal of unknown and highly variable characteristics. An audio signal generator (Fig. 4-18) should be used for making modulation-level, distortion, and frequency-response measurements.

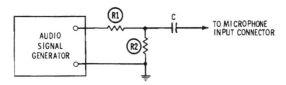

(A) Carbon-microphone arrangement.

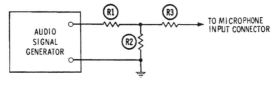

(B) High-impedance microphone arrangement.

Fig. 4-18. Audio signal-generator connections.

When connecting an audio signal generator to a CB set designed for use with a carbon microphone, the arrangement shown in Fig. 4-18A may be used. Resistors R1 and R2 form a voltage divider and a load for the signal generator. If the signal generator is designed to work into a 1,000-ohm load, R1 can be 1,000 ohms and R2, 20 ohms. Capacitor C, which prevents shorting of the microphone excitation voltage, can have a value of around .02 mfd.

Since a much smaller audio signal is required when the CB set is designed for use with a high-impedance dynamic, ceramic or crystal microphone, the arrangement shown in Fig. 4-18B should be used. Here again, R1 and R2 form a voltage divider and a load for the generator. The value of R1 should be the same as the intended signal-generator load impedance (usually 1,000 or 2,000 ohms), and R2 should be a 1-ohm resistor. R3 may be of almost any value between 100,000 ohms and one megohm. If the signal is too small, try a resistor of smaller value for R3.

The standard test frequency is 1,000 cps. Set the audio signal-generator output to zero and, with the transmitter turned on (connected to a dummy antenna load), gradually increase the generator output. Connect an oscilloscope to the plate of the modulator tube and observe the waveform; it should be a relatively clean sine wave if the signal-generator output is a sine wave. A wave analyzer can be used to measure distortion.

The actual modulated radio carrier may be observed on a scope screen by connecting the scope vertical input to the plate of the last IF amplifier of another CB set (Fig. 4-19) that is tuned to the frequency of the transmitter being tested. To prevent overloading of the test receiver, do not connect it to an antenna or, better yet, terminate its antenna connector in a dummy load.

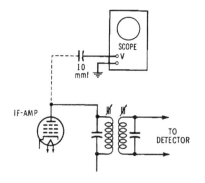

Fig. 4-19. Scope connection for modulator check.

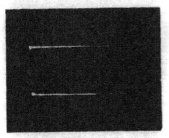

(A) Unmodulated RF carrier.

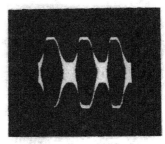

(B) Undermodulated RF carrier.

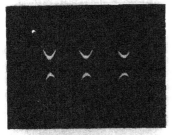

(C) Typical modulated carrier.

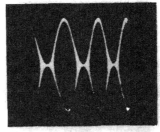

(D) 100% modulated carrier.

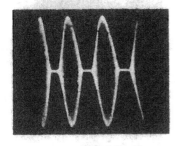

(E) Overmodulated carrier.

Fig. 4-20. Scope modulation-test patterns.

With the transmitter turned on, but with the modulating signal turned off, adjust the scope so that you see a pattern similar to that shown in Fig. 4-20A. The individual RF cycles may not be visible unless your scope is a wide-band type.

Now apply the tone signal to the transmitter microphone input and note that the waveform looks like the pattern shown in Fig. 4-20C. Raise and lower the audio-signal level to note the range of modulation capability, referring to the reference patterns in Figs. 4-20B to 4-20D. Overmodulation, as shown in Fig. 4-20E, should not be allowed to occur, particularly when using a microphone. Tune the signal generator through the 300-3,000-cps range and observe the relative modulation percentage with respect to 1,000 cps. Above 3,000 cps, the modulation level should drop off.

To test for modulation symmetry, make the same test as that just described, except with the horizontal gain of the scope set to zero—you should see a straight vertical line. With the modulating signal turned off, adjust the scope so that the middle of the line is at the horizontal reference line. Now, as you turn up the audio-signal input, the line should become longer and should extend an equal distance above and below the reference line if the modulation is symmetrical.

The same tests can be performed using the microphone as the audio-signal source. Talking into the microphone should cause the vertical line to expand equally upward and downward from the reference point. With the scope horizontal gain advanced to cause the sweep to fill the screen, you should see the pattern of your voice riding the top and bottom of the RF carrier. When trying new microphones, you can use these techniques to determine which have adequate or excessive output for the set being serviced.

A CB receiver is used as a frequency converter when using a scope to make these modulation checks. The RF carrier frequency is too high to be fed directly into a typical scope.

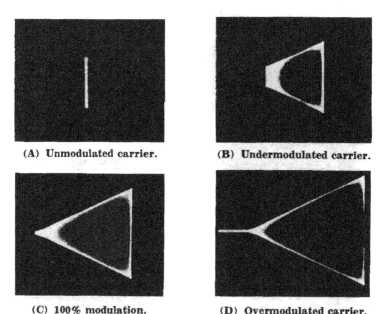

(A) Unmodulated carrier. (B) Undermodulated carrier.

(C) 100% modulation. (D) Overmodulated carrier.

Fig. 4-21. Trapezoidal modulation-test patterns.

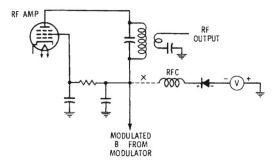

Fig. 4-22. Overmodulation-detection circuit.

When a CB set is used as explained, the receiver heterodynes the 27-mc band signal down to a frequency within the range of a relatively low-cost scope.

The trapezoid-pattern method of measuring modulation is also widely used, but it requires more time and effort. Typically, the modulated RF signal is fed directly to the scope vertical-deflection plates, and the output of the modulator is connected to the horizontal input of the scope. When this technique is used, the patterns shown in Fig. 4-21, should be obtained.

Overmodulation can be checked without a scope by connecting a DC voltmeter to the output of the modulator (Fig. 4-22). The RF choke may be of any convenient value. The diode must be one whose PIV rating is several hundred volts and must be connected as shown to prevent positive B+ from flowing through the meter. Note the meter polarity shown in the diagram.

When talking loudly into the microphone, the meter should indicate zero. If overmodulation peaks occur, the meter needle will "kick."

REPLACING COMPONENTS

When available, the modulation reactor-output transformer should be replaced only with one supplied by the manufacturer of the CB set or an exact electrical duplicate. This is especially important when the design of this component is related to the design of the rest of the frequency response and overmodulation protection. When an exact replacement is not available and the most similar part available is used, measurements should be made to determine that original performance is equalled or bettered.

Capacitors, resistors, and tubes should be replaced with like types, not necessarily of the same manufacture. Ceramic capacitors, for example, should not be replaced by paper dielectric or other types, because there are electrical differences among capacitors of the same rated capacitance and voltage. The selection made by the engineer who designed the equipment is nearly always based on valid reasons. When some other type of component is used as a replacement, the equipment might no longer perform as specified.

Chapter 5

Selectivity and Sensitivity

A Citizens band receiver must have a great deal of gain in order to receive radio signals of only a few microvolts and deliver a watt or more of audio power. The sensitivity of a CB receiver is normally rated as the number of microvolts of signal at the antenna terminals for a specified (usually 10 db) signal-to-noise ratio. If, for example, the receiver is rated at 1 microvolt for a 10-db signal-to-noise ratio, the audio signal output is 10 db greater than the noise output when an RF signal is applied at a level of 1 microvolt.

RECEIVER GAIN

The actual gain of the receiver is determined by the strength of the signal required to produce full-rated audio output. If a 10-microvolt radio signal is required to produce 1 watt of audio into a 3.2-ohm speaker, the voltage gain of the receiver is 179,000, the ratio of 0.00001 volts (10 microvolts) to 1.79 volts (output voltage = $\sqrt{1 \text{ watt} \times 3.2 \text{ ohms}}$). The power gain in decibels can be calculated by determining the power input in dbw (db below 1 watt) by dividing the square of the input voltage (10 microvolts squared) by the load resistance (generally 50 ohms), and then converting the ratio of input power and output power (1 watt) into db.

This great amount of amplification is required in order to make effective use of low-power CB signals. While receivers that have even greater gain can be designed, no useful purpose is served since the ambient noise level limits useful sensitivity. Under good conditions, the ambient background noise is in the order of 2-3 microvolts or more in the 27-mc band. Gain control will be discussed later.

Superregenerative Receivers

Very simple receivers used in early CB sets have amazingly

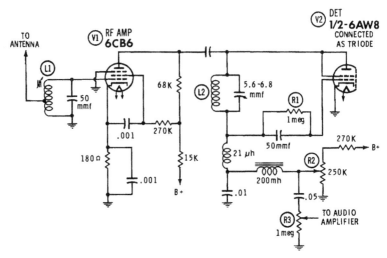

Fig. 5-1. Superregenerative CB receiver.

high sensitivity for the number of tubes used. A superregenerative detector, utilizing only one tube, is capable of operating with radio signals of only a few microvolts and is almost as sensitive as a superheterodyne-type receiver using several tubes. However, superregenerative receivers have other limitations that limit their use.

A superregenerative detector generates a radio signal which is radiated if the antenna is fed directly to the detector circuit. Therefore, an RF-amplifier stage is generally used between the detector and the antenna, as shown in Fig. 5-1. The antenna is fed to a tap on coil L1 and the amplified signal is capacitively coupled to detector coil L2.

Grid leak R1 is connected so that a positive DC bias is applied to the detector (shown in the diagram) to produce the desired superregenerative effect. If R1 were connected between grid and ground, the detector would be regenerative instead of superregenerative. Its sensitivity would be reduced, and its selectivity would be greatly improved, but it would be more difficult for a novice to operate. Sensitivity is controlled by R2, which varies detector plate voltage; R1 is the audio volume control.

Superheterodyne Receivers

Most CB sets employ superheterodyne-type receivers to obtain the required sensitivity and high selectivity. In this type receiver as explained in Chapter 3, the incoming radio signal is converted to a lower frequency where it is easier to obtain gain and selectivity. Many receivers employ single-conversion superheterodyne circuits in which the signal frequency is heterodyned but once to a lower frequency. Others utilize a dual-conversion superheterodyne circuit in which the signal frequency is heterodyned to a lower frequency in two steps. In some sophisticated communications receivers, triple conversion is used.

A superheterodyne receiver always contains at least one mixer (first detector), a local oscillator, an IF amplifier, and a demodulator (second detector) ahead of the audio amplifier. Dual-conversion receivers employ two mixers and two local oscillators. In any type of superheterodyne receiver, one or more RF-amplifier stages can precede the first mixer, and more than one IF-amplifier stage at the same frequency is sometimes used.

ANTENNA-INPUT CIRCUITS

The same antenna is generally used with a CB set for transmitting and receiving. In some sets, a relay or switch is used to connect the antenna alternately to the transmitter output and receiver input, as shown in Fig. 5-2. The radiating element of the antenna is connected through the center conductor of the antenna transmission line (coaxial cable) to the antenna switch or relay. The coaxial cable shield connects the antenna ground plane (or sleeve) to the CB set chassis ground. The shield minimizes unwanted pick-up of radio signals and noise by the transmission line.

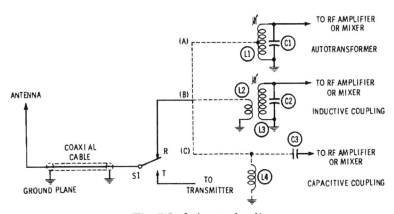

Fig. 5-2. Antenna circuits.

In Fig. 5-2, the ungrounded side of the antenna circuit may be fed to a tap of the receiver antenna coil (L1), as shown in A; to the primary winding (L2) of an antenna transformer (L2-L3), as shown in B; or through a capacitor (C3), as shown in C. In this case, the antenna circuit is usually loaded by a coil (L4).

Typical RF-amplifier antenna input circuits are shown in Figs. 5-3, 5-4, 5-5, 5-6, and 5-7. One of the more commonly used circuits is shown in Fig. 5-3. Here, the antenna is

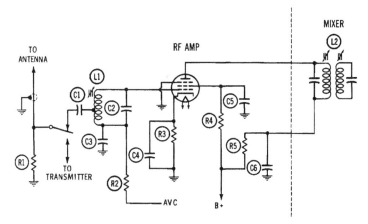

Fig. 5-3. Tapped coil input.

grounded through R1, a resistor ranging in value from 1,000 ohms to 470,000 ohms. Its purpose is to drain off static charges on the antenna without significant loss of radio signal. This is not present in all receivers.

The signal from the antenna is fed through C1, whose value is not critical, to a tap on antenna coil L1. The RF signal is applied across the portion of L1 below the tap because C3, in effect, grounds the bottom of L1. Since L1 is an autotransformer, the signal voltage across C2 is considerably higher than the applied voltage. The autotransformer functions both as a voltage step-up transformer and as an impedance-matching device which makes it possible to terminate the 50-ohm antenna transmission line into the coil without greatly lowering the Q of the tuned circuit (L1-C2). The slug of L1 is tuned for optimum operation on the channels to be received. Since the bottom of L1 is not grounded directly (it is grounded for RF through C3), the DC AVC voltage can be applied to the grid through L1.

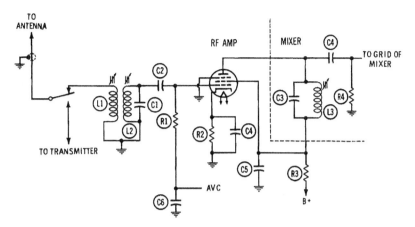

Fig. 5-4. Separate input coil.

A separate antenna coil is used in the circuit shown in Fig. 5-4. The signal developed across L1 is inductively coupled to L2. The transformer (L1-L2) serves as an impedance-matching device in a manner similar to that of the autotransformer in Fig. 5-3. However, the manner in which AVC voltage is fed to the grid of the tube differs between the two circuits. In Fig. 5-4, capacitor C2 isolates L2 for DC, but passes RF, making it possible to feed the AVC voltage to the grid through R1, which can be of such high value as to cause negligible loading of the tuned circuit.

Switchless Antenna Circuits

No antenna switch or relay is used in the circuits shown in Figs. 5-5, 5-6, and 5-7. The incoming RF signal (Fig. 5-4) is developed across L1, the antenna coupling winding of the transmitter output circuit. The signal is capacitively coupled to the receiver RF amplifier through a low-value capacitor which does not significantly load down the tuned circuit (L3-C3). Resistor R1 across the tuned circuit broadens the resonance and minimizes any effect the tuning of L3-C3 might have on the transmitter tank (L1-L2).

Here, AVC voltage is fed through the tuned circuit, which is placed at RF ground potential by C4. Resistor R2 serves as one arm of a voltage divider that reduces the AVC voltage to the desired level, and limits the grid current that flows during transmission because of the presence of the strong transmitter signal. The transmitter signal does not affect the

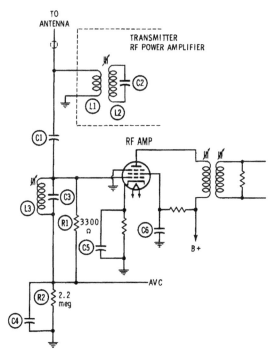

Fig. 5-5. Capacitance input.

rest of the receiver since the local oscillator plate voltage is cut off during transmission.

A series-resonant wave trap (C1-L1) is shunted across the antenna (Fig. 5-6). It is tuned to approximately 54 mc to reduce transmission of second harmonics which could cause interference to nearby TV receivers. When receiving, the wave trap attenuates signals in the vicinity of 54 mc which might desensitize the receiver.

The incoming RF signal is developed across L2 and inductively coupled to L3. The signal across L3 is capacitively coupled through C4 to the grid of the RF-amplifier tube. In this circuit, L2 and L3 are shared by the transmitter and receiver.

AVC voltage is fed through R1 to the RF-amplifier grid. The bottom of R1 is placed at RF ground potential by C5. In addition to AVC voltage, which varies with the strength of the incoming signals, the self bias (cathode bias) applied to the RF-amplifier tube can be adjusted by sensitivity control R2.

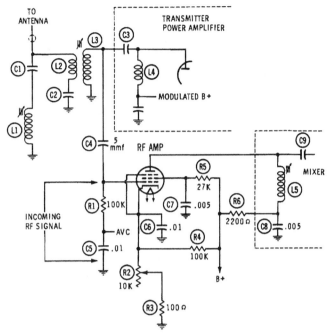

Fig. 5-6. Common transmit-receive tank.

Pi-Network Input Circuit—A pi-network is shared by the transmitter and receiver in the circuit shown in Fig. 5-7. In this circuit a resistor (R1) is shunted across the antenna to bleed off static charges. A series-resonant wave trap (L1-C1) is also shunted across the antenna to reduce second harmonic emission during transmission.

An in-band incoming RF signal ignores the wave trap and is fed through the pi-network (C2-L2-C3) to the grid of the RF amplifier through C6. The pi-network is resonant at the CB frequencies and also acts as an impedance matcher and as a low-pass filter which attenuates unwanted signals at frequencies above the Citizens band.

Antenna Circuit Troubles

When a relay or switch is used to transfer the antenna from the receiver to the transmitter, troubles may be caused by dirty or defective switch or relay contacts. These contacts should be kept clean, but never filed; sufficient pressure between the contacts must be maintained. Low-tension switches or relays should be replaced.

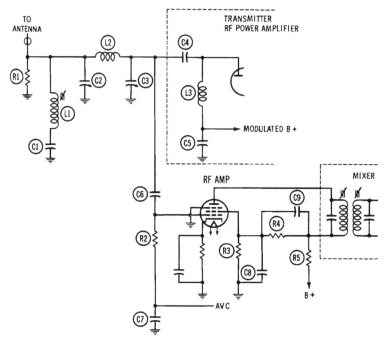

Fig. 5-7. Pi-network input.

RF AMPLIFIERS

The main purpose of an RF amplifier in a CB set is to increase the gain or sensitivity of the receiver. Its secondary purpose may be to improve the selectivity of the receiver in terms of image signal rejection and attenuation of other out-of-band signals. In a receiver to be used for reception on one channel only, the RF amplifier may also improve selectivity in terms of rejection of adjacent CB channel signals. Most CB sets are designed for multichannel operation and the RF amplifier must be broadly tuned to favor the entire band, and not sharply resonant to any particular channel frequency.

While more than one RF-amplifier stage could be used ahead of the mixer, there would be little to gain in CB operations because the added sensitivity is not needed and the improved selectivity would be detrimental when multichannel operation is used. Furthermore, there is danger of over-driving the mixer and the second RF amplifier stage by strong signals. This could result in the production of unwanted modulation products.

84

Even when only a single RF-amplifier stage is used ahead of the mixer, the circuit must be designed to minimize harmful effects that could be caused by strong adjacent and co-channel signals, which the tuned circuits are not designed to reject. The chore of providing the required rejection of adjacent and co-channel signals (selectivity) is passed on to the IF amplifier.

RF Amplifier Tubes

In nearly all CB receivers equipped with an RF amplifier, a remote cut-off pentode is used in the RF-amplifier stage. The gain of the tube is varied automatically by the AVC voltage and can be reduced permanently to minimize the effects of strong adjacent and co-channel signals. This is accomplished by replacing the screen-voltage dropping resistor with one of higher value or by increasing the value of the cathode resistor.

Sensitivity Control

In most of the circuits shown previously, a fixed cathode resistor is used to provide minimum bias when AVC voltage is very low; but in the circuit of Fig. 5-6, note that the minimum bias level can be set by adjusting R2, which is connected in a voltage divider circuit. The cathode is made positive with respect to the grid by a voltage divider consisting of R4, R2, and R3. Increasing the value of R2 raises the bias voltage, and vice versa. The bias voltage also increases as AVC voltage decreases, since cathode current flows through R2 and bias range-limiting resistor R3.

The RF gain control (R2) is a built-in feature of the *Courier* 1 Transceiver which makes it possible to reduce sensitivity when full gain is not required and to reduce the effects of strong adjacent and co-channel signals. A gain control can be added to receivers not equipped with this feature by connecting a 10,000-ohm potentiometer in series with the RF-amplifier cathode resistor.

Tuned Circuits

Because of low cost and small size, most receivers employ slug-tuned coils which may or may not be shunted by low-value fixed capacitors. Some sets employ fixed coils, with an air-core or a ferrite-core, shunted by a variable capacitor that is the tuning adjustment.

RF-Amplifier Troubles

When coils with tuning slugs or fixed ferrite cores are used, the core or slug may get jarred out of place due to shock or vibration during use in a vehicle or shipment—this kind of trouble may be hard to trace. If adjustment of a tuning slug has practically no effect on receiver performance, look for an open capacitor across the coil (if one is used) or a misplaced core or slug. A grid-dip meter, with its coil placed close to the coil being checked, may come in handy for determining whether the coil has a shorted turn or misplaced core or slug by noting the frequency at which the coil is resonant. Sometimes the coil is used in a circuit which is not resonant in the band, and the coil serves mainly as a high impedance over a broad band of frequencies.

Lack of adequate gain in an RF amplifier is sometimes caused by an open bypass capacitor at the screen grid, AVC return, cathode, or plate return. Since we are working near the high end of the HF (high-frequency band) and at the border of the VHF band, capacitors used in the RF-amplifier circuit should be replaced only by new ones of identical capacity, and preferably one of the same make and type. Ordinary paper tubular capacitors might have excessive inductance at these frequencies, and hence may not be effective bypasses.

MIXER CIRCUITS

Mixer is just another term for what used to be called the "first detector" when superheterodyne receivers first appeared. It is also called a *converter* or *frequency translator*. Regardless of what it is called, it is a sort of detector since it is a nonlinear device. Its output voltage is not linear with its input voltage, as is the case with Class-A amplifiers.

When two or more signals are applied simultaneously to the grid of a tube (biased to be nonlinear), the composite signal at the plate contains not only signals at the input-signal frequencies, but also signals at frequencies which are equal to the sum and difference of the input signals. Other signals, such as harmonics of the input signals, may also appear at the output.

Simple Mixers

Crystal diodes are used in radar receivers and microwave communications receivers as mixers to *mix* the incoming signal with a locally generated signal to form an intermediate-

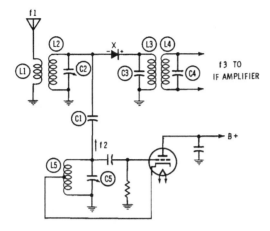

Fig. 5-8. Crystal mixer.

frequency (IF) signal which can be more readily amplified than the original microwave signal. The same techniques can be used at lower frequencies.

A hypothetical circuit of a crystal mixer is shown in Fig. 5-8. The incoming signal (f1) is passed through a filter (L1-L2-C2) that is resonant at f1, then to the crystal diode. A locally generated signal at frequency f2 is also fed through C1 to the crystal diode. Frequencies f1 and f2 appear across L3-C3, but are very low in amplitude since L3-C3-L4-C4 is a filter designed to pass only one of the beat frequencies produced by mixing f1 and f2. If these tuned circuits are resonant to the difference between f1 and f2, a new frequency, f3, equal to f1 − f2, appears across L4-C4 and all other frequencies are greatly attenuated.

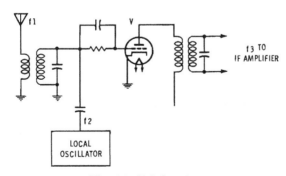

Fig. 5-9. Triode mixer.

Triode Mixers

A triode tube can also be used as a mixer (Fig. 5-9). The mixer triode, in this case, is operated as a grid-leak detector. Its output circuit is tuned to the desired beat frequency (f1 + f2 or f1 – f2) caused by mixing f1 and f2.

Tetrode and Pentode Mixers

Tetrode and pentode tubes may also be used as mixers, provided they are biased (usually by the cathode resistor) as nonlinear devices.

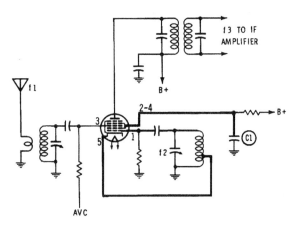

Fig. 5-10. Pentagrid converter.

Pentagrid Converters

Special tubes are widely used which contain the mixer and local oscillator in one tube envelope. A pentagrid converter circuit is shown in Fig. 5-10. Here, the local oscillator (f2), shown in heavy lines, utilizes the cathode, grid No. 1 and grid No. 2 as a triode in a Hartley circuit. Grid No. 2 functions as the plate. The incoming signal (f1) is fed to grid No. 3, which is between grid No. 2 and grid No. 4, which are both at a positive DC potential, but at ground potential for RF because of capacitor C1. Grid No. 3 modulates the electron stream, which is already modulated by the oscillator but is otherwise isolated from the oscillator. Grid No. 5 is a suppressor grid and operates the same as in a pentode. Since grid No. 1 modulates the electron stream at f2 and grid No. 3 modulates the electron stream at f1, both f1, f2, and their

88

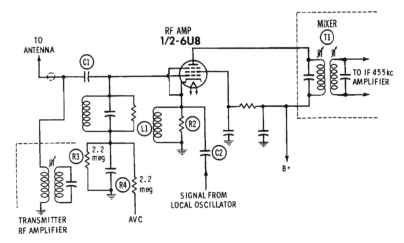

Fig. 5-11. Pentode CB mixer fed from antenna.

beats appear in the plate circuit. By tuning the plate circuit to f3 (the sum or difference of f1 and f2), the original frequencies and undesired beat frequency are attenuated and the desired beat frequency is fed to the IF amplifier. If one or the other of the two signals to be mixed is modulated (AM or FM), the resulting beat signals will also be modulated.

Typical CB Mixers

In the Heathkit Model GW-11A, the antenna is fed directly to the mixer grid through C1 (Fig. 5-11) since no RF ampli-

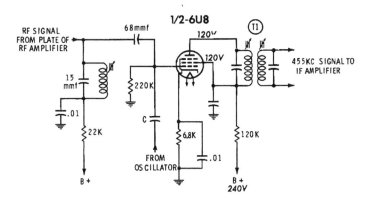

Fig. 5-12. Pentode CB mixer fed from RF amplifier.

89

fier stage is used. The local oscillator signal is fed through C2 to the cathode of the tube and is developed across L1, a 30-uh RF choke that is shunted by R2. Since L1 has very low DC resistance, practically no DC cathode bias is developed.

The mixer tube is biased by the variable AVC voltage, but at a lower level than the IF amplifier. The AVC voltage is cut in half by the voltage divider (R3-R4). The plate circuit is fed through 455 kc IF transformer T1.

A similar mixer (Fig. 5-12) used in the Kaar TR327B employs an RF stage ahead of the mixer. Here the local oscillator signal is fed to the mixer grid instead of the cathode. The tube bias voltage is higher than normal and the plate and screen are operated at reduced voltage to obtain the desired results.

Both of the mixers described are used in single-conversion superheterodyne receivers. A similar circuit is used in the first mixer stage of the double conversion Hammarlund CB-23, as shown in Fig. 5-13. Both the received signal, from the plate of the RF amplifier, and the local-oscillator signal are capacitively coupled to the same grid of the mixer tube.

Pentagrid Second Mixer

Pentagrid-type mixers are widely used in the second mixer stage. In the Vocaline ED-27M, a 6BE6 tube is used as the second mixer and second local oscillator in a circuit similar

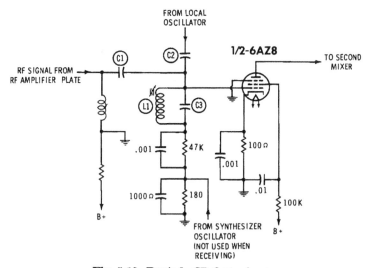

Fig. 5-13. Pentode CB first mixer.

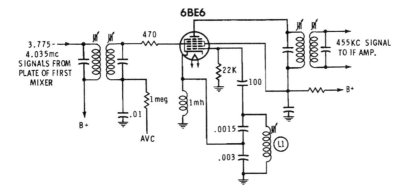

Fig. 5-14. Pentagrid second mixer with self-excited second oscillator.

to that shown in Fig. 5-14. The RF amplifier and first mixer (not shown) are broadly tuned to the Citizens band. The first local oscillator is crystal controlled at one frequency only, 31 mc. When the 31-mc signal is mixed with incoming CB signals in the first mixer, the output of the mixer contains various beat signals in the 3.775-4.035-mc range. Selection of the desired channel is made at the second mixer by means of a switch that selects any one of four coils in the self-excited second local-oscillator circuit. (Only one coil, L1, is shown in the diagram.) Each oscillator coil is tuned so that a 455-kc beat signal is produced in the output of the second mixer only when the beat signal from the first mixer represents the desired CB channel.

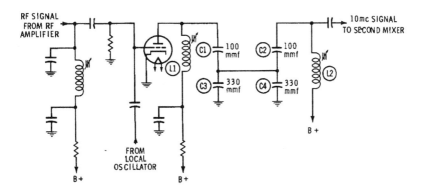

Fig. 5-15. Triode first mixer with bandpass output filter.

91

Triode Mixers

A triode is used in the first mixer stage of the dual-conversion Executive Model 50. As shown in Fig. 5-15, the first local oscillator signal is fed through a capacitor to the grid of the triode along with the incoming CB signal. The resulting 10-mc beat signal is fed to the second mixer through a capacitively coupled bandpass filter (L1-C1-C2-C3-C4-L2).

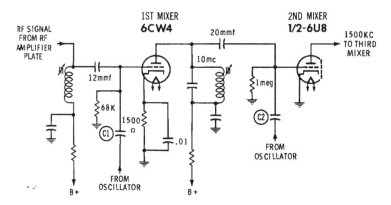

Fig. 5-16. Cascaded triode mixers.

Two triode mixers follow one another in the Courier 1 Transceiver (Fig. 5-16). The output of the first mixer is 10 mc and the output of the second mixer is 1,500 kc. The output of the third mixer (not shown), which employs a pentagrid converter tube, is at 262 kc.

SELECTIVITY AHEAD OF THE IF AMPLIFIER

Various types of RF-amplifier and mixer circuits have been shown to illustrate how incoming CB signals are pre-amplified and heterodyned prior to high amplification at a relatively low frequency. In all of these circuits some selectivity, as well as voltage gain, is obtained.

The stages ahead of the final IF-amplifier section introduce selectivity mainly in the form of rejection of image signals and other unwanted out-of-band signals.

Image Signals

In a single-conversion receiver with a 455-kc IF, signals are heard that are either 455 kc above or below the frequency at which the local oscillator is operating. For example, if the oscillator is operating at 26.620 mc or 27.530 mc, the receiver will be most sensitive to incoming signals at 27.075 mc. With the oscillator operating at 26.620 mc, a receiver which normally receives signals at 27.075 mc (27.075 mc − 26.620 mc = 455 kc) may also accept incoming signals at 26.165 mc, since a 26.165-mc signal mixed with a 26.620-mc signal also produces a 455-kc IF signal. It is the job of the RF-amplifier and mixer tuning circuits to attenuate the 26.165-mc signal and to pass the desired 27.075-mc signal.

On the other hand, if the oscillator operates at 27.530 mc when the receiver is set to receive on 27.075 mc, the receiver may also pick up signals on 27.985 mc, since mixing 27.985 mc and 27.530 mc also produces a 455-kc IF signal.

If the receiver IF is at a higher frequency, such as 1,650 kc, the image is farther away from the Citizens band and is subject to more attenuation by the RF and mixer tuned circuits. When the local oscillator operates 1,650 kc above the desired CB channel frequency, the image is at 29.375 mc; and when it is 1,650 kc below, the image is at 23.775 mc.

By making the IF as high as possible, image rejection is improved, but at the sacrifice of gain and in-band selectivity. In dual- and triple-conversion receivers, excellent image rejection is attained without sacrificing gain and in-band selectivity.

Eliminating Image Interference—When image interference occurs frequently, one cure is to replace the CB set with one that has a different IF. But, after doing so, an image signal might be present at another frequency. The elimination of image interference is relatively easy when using a single-channel receiver—change operating frequencies or add a wave trap. When multichannel operation is employed, the problem can become rather involved.

When a series-resonant wave trap connected across the antenna terminals (Fig. 5-6) is tuned to the frequency of the interfering signal, it should do the trick in most cases.

Role of IF Amplifiers

The backbone of the CB receiver is the IF amplifier, which narrows the bandpass of the receiver so that it will give preference to a single channel and tend to reject signals on adjacent channels. Because of the narrow bandwidth and relatively low frequency, it is easy to get considerable gain using low-cost components.

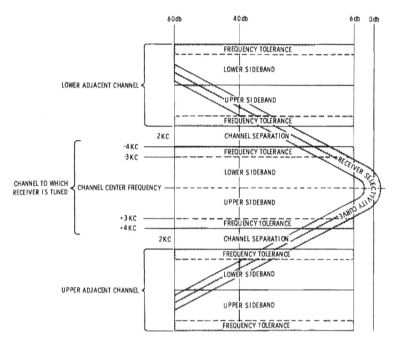

Fig. 5-17. Selectivity curve of double conversion receiver superimposed on three adjacent channels.

Selectivity Problem

In a multichannel receiver, the RF amplifier and mixer are supposed to pass the entire 300-kc band of frequencies in the 26.960-27.260-mc range (Citizens band). Ideally, the IF amplifier is supposed to pass a band only a little more than 8 kc wide (two 3-kc sidebands and two 1-kc frequency-tolerance guard bands).

No CB receiver has a rectangular selective curve. Instead, the selectivity curve of a high-grade dual-conversion superheterodyne CB receiver is shown in Fig. 5-17. Its relationship to an on-frequency signal and two adjacent channels of equal strength are illustrated. The curve is not a narrow line, but shifts up or down in frequency as much or even more than 1 kc because of variations in local oscillator frequency.

The sidebands of an AM signal contain only a part of the radiated power so that the picture is not as black as it seems. Also, a strong signal on the desired frequency reduces the sensitivity of the receiver to adjacent channel signals because of AVC action. Nevertheless, it is apparent that interference from adjacent channel stations should be expected at times.

94

The ability of CB receivers to reject adjacent channel signals can be improved through the use of more sophisticated filters ahead of or within the IF amplifiers, but only a few users are willing to pay the added cost.

Typical IF Amplifiers

The IF amplifiers are essentially the same in all CB receivers. Most have one IF stage (some have two) and nearly all employ IF transformers with adjustable cores for tuning. A typical IF-amplifier stage is shown in Fig. 5-18. Usually, T1

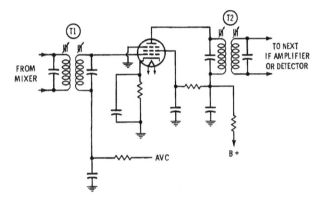

Fig. 5-18. Typical IF amplifier stage.

and T2 are identical. Sometimes the IF transformer feeding the detector is of special design. Selectivity is achieved by relatively loose coupling between IF amplifier transformer windings, high-Q circuits and peak tuning of all circuits. In contrast, TV and FM broadcast-receiver IF amplifiers are intentionally broad band by design.

IF-Amplifier Troubles

Aside from outright failure of components, IF amplifiers are prone to self-oscillation when gain is high; this may be caused by changes in values of components and improper dressing of leads.

DETECTOR CIRCUITS

The detector (as differentiated from mixer stages) generally is of a type that contributes no gain. While there are detector

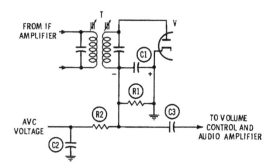

Fig. 5-19. Basic diode detector.

circuits that contribute gain, they are not as practical to use as the standard diode detector circuit shown in Fig. 5-19. The IF signal appearing across the secondary of IF transformer T is applied to the diode and load resistor R1, which are in series. The diode rectifies the AC signal voltage, causing a DC voltage (polarity noted in diagram) and the audio component of the signal to develop across R1. Capacitor C1 removes any remaining RF. The audio signal is fed through C3 to the audio amplifier, generally through a volume control.

The DC voltage appearing across R1 is also utilized to automatically control the gain of the receiver (AVC) by feeding it to the grids of RF and IF amplifier tubes. Resistor R2 isolates the AVC circuit from the audio circuit, and capacitor C2 prevents the AVC voltage from varying with the audio signal.

RECEIVER ALIGNMENT

To achieve maximum sensitivity and selectivity, the tuned circuits of the receiver must be correctly aligned with respect to each other. The procedures for aligning CB receivers are essentially the same as for other AM superheterodyne receivers. The alignment process, unless specified in the set instruction book, is from the output to the input. That is, the IF transformer feeding the detector is tuned first, then the preceding IF transformer, and so on until the antenna stage is reached. The following procedure is standard for single-conversion superheterodyne receivers.

1. Connect an AC voltmeter across the speaker terminals to monitor the audio-output voltage level.
2. Disable the local oscillator, if it is of the fixed-tuned,

96

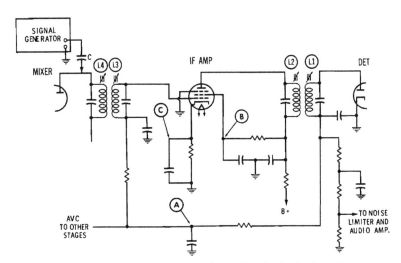

Fig. 5-20. Signal level monitoring points in typical receiver.

crystal-controlled type by removing the receiver crystal or setting the channel selector to an unused channel.

3. Connect the hot output lead of an RF-signal generator to the plate of the mixer tube through a small capacitor, about 10 mmf capacity (Fig. 5-20), and the ground lead to the set chassis.

4. Set the signal generator to produce a modulated signal at the receiver IF (usually 455 kc or 1,650 kc) and set the output attenuator to a very low level.

5. Increase the signal-generator output level until the tone modulation is heard in the set speaker with the receiver volume and squelch controls "full on" and the noise limiter cut out of the circuit.

6. Set the AC voltmeter so that the audio-output level can be read easily.

7. Adjust the detector IF transformer (L1, L2 in Fig. 5-20) and then the preceding IF transformer (L3, L4), or transformers, for maximum meter reading. Reduce the signal generator output and retune the IF transformers for maximum meter reading.

8. Remove the hot signal-generator lead from the mixer plate and drape the lead around the mixer tube, increasing signal generator output if necessary, and retrim L4 (plate load of mixer). This corrects for any detuning effect the signal generator lead may have had when it was connected to the mixer plate.

9. Reactivate the local oscillator by reinserting the crystal or setting the channel selector to an active channel.
10. Connect the signal-generator output lead to the set antenna connector (ground lead still connected to the chassis).
11. Adjust the signal generator output to the receiver operating frequency (in CB band) with modulation on. Tune the signal generator slowly for maximum-output meter reading. Reduce the signal-generator output to the minimum level required to obtain a meter reading.
12. Adjust the mixer-input trimmers and RF-amplifier trimmers for maximum meter reading, reducing signal-generator output as necessary.
13. If the set is of the multichannel type, repeat step 12 for each channel and compromise-tune mixer and RF-amplifier trimmers for uniform-as-possible output meter reading on all channels. If the receiver is of the tunable type, trim first at 27.255 mc, then at 26.965 mc and retrim for best average performance across the band.
14. Disconnect the signal generator and connect the set to an antenna. Retune the antenna trimmer *only* for best reception on a weak on-the-air signal, averaged for all channels, using your ear as the output monitor.

Aligning Dual-Conversion Sets

Alignment of dual-conversion superheterodyne receivers requires a few more steps. Perform Steps 1 through 8, but de-activate both local oscillators. Then re-activate the second local oscillator, apply a signal at the high IF to the plate of the first mixer, and tune up the second mixer input circuits. Re-activate the first local oscillator and perform Steps 9 through 14.

Aligning Triple-Conversion Sets

To align a triple-conversion superheterodyne receiver, read the applicable instruction book carefully, since special procedures may be applicable. In general, perform Steps 1 through 8, with all three local oscillators disabled. Then re-activate the third local oscillator, feed a signal at the mid IF to the plate of the second mixer and align the third mixer input circuits. Re-activate the second local oscillator, apply a signal at the high IF to the plate of the first mixer, and align the second mixer input circuits. Re-activate the first local oscillator and perform steps 9 through 14.

De-activating Oscillators

Sometimes it is not easy to de-activate all of the local oscillators. Pulling oscillator tubes out of their sockets may alter the receiver filament voltages if the tube filaments are connected in series-parallel. Some local oscillators are not crystal controlled and cannot be de-activated by removing a crystal. When aligning IF stages with local oscillators functioning, be careful not to tune up the set to a spurious signal caused by beating of various signals in the set.

Alignment Metering

While the use of an AC voltmeter to monitor audio-output voltage when aligning a receiver is easy, you can monitor AVC voltage or the effects of AVC voltage instead. You can connect a DC VTVM to point A in Fig. 5-20 to monitor AVC voltage directly. This voltage will be negative with respect to ground, and an improvement in alignment will be indicated by an *increase* in AVC voltage.

You can also connect a DC voltmeter to point B in Fig. 5-22, the screen grid of the IF amplifier. This voltage will be positive with respect to ground, and an improvement in alignment will be indicated by an *increase* in screen voltage. A DC voltmeter connected to point C, the cathode of the IF amplifier, will be positive with respect to ground, and an improvement in alignment will be indicated by a *decrease* in cathode voltage.

When monitoring AVC, screen or cathode voltage, an unmodulated signal can be used.

Sensitivity Measurement

You can measure the sensitivity of a CB receiver if you have a high-grade signal generator whose output attenuators truly indicate the actual level of the output signal. Inexpensive signal generators may be equipped with calibrated attenuators, but the leakage through the case and past the attenuators may be great enough to lead to erroneous conclusions.

Sensitivity is measured by feeding a signal of known level to the receiver input and measuring the receiver output level. The method of connecting the signal generator to the receiver input depends on the output impedance or termination ar-

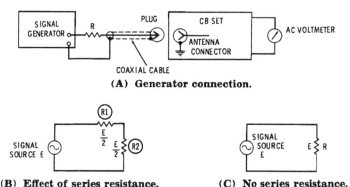

(A) Generator connection.

(B) Effect of series resistance.   (C) No series resistance.
Fig. 5-21. Signal generator arrangements.

rangements of the signal generator. A typical setup is shown
in Fig. 5-21A.

Here the signal is fed to the CB set antenna terminal
through a piece of coaxial cable and a 50-ohm series resistor,
as shown in Fig. 5-21A. The equivalent circuit is shown in
Fig. 5-21B, where R1 represents the 50-ohm series resistor
and R2 the 50-ohm receiver input impedance. The signal
voltage fed to the receiver is half of the value indicated by
the signal-generator attenuators. On the other hand, if the
signal-generator output is fed directly to the receiver input,
indicated as R in Fig. 5-21C, the signal voltage is the indicated
full value if the proper impedance match is obtained.

To measure sensitivity, set the CB receiver volume and
squelch controls wide open (noise limiter off), tune the signal
generator carefully to the receiver operating frequency (in
Citizens band), as indicated by maximum reading on the AC
voltmeter connected across the speaker. The signal should be
amplitude modulated 30% at 400 cps or 1,000 cps. Adjust
the signal-generator output to produce an audible audio tone
in the speaker. Now turn the signal on and off while adjusting
the signal-generator output level. At the point where the modulated signal produces a meter reading 10 db higher than that
noted when the signal is not present, note the signal-generator
attenuator settings. If your meter is calibrated in decibels, you
can read the 10-db difference in output levels directly.

If the signal-generator attenuators indicate that the output
is 2 microvolts and there is no series resistor between the
signal generator and receiver, you can assume that the re-

100

ceiver sensitivity is approximately 2 microvolts for a 10-db signal-to-noise ratio. If a series resistor is used, the attenuators will indicate 4 microvolts for 2-microvolt sensitivity.

Receiver Gain Measurement

With the apparatus connected as described, adjust the signal-generator output (modulated signal) until the output meter indicates that 1 watt of audio is being produced. If the speaker impedance is 3.2 ohms, the AC voltmeter reading should be 1.7 volts. The receiver can be said to be capable of delivering 1 watt of audio with an input signal of so many microvolts. To determine the gain in decibels, it is necessary to convert microvolts across 50 ohms into terms of watts which can be translated into the db difference between input and output.

Selectivity Measurements

The same setup can be used for measuring selectivity. One way to measure relative selectivity is as follows. Tune the signal generator to the receiver operating frequency and apply a modulated signal at a level that produces 50 milliwatts audio output (0.4 volt AC across 3.2-ohm speaker). Then double the signal generator output voltage (6 db) and tune it above the receiver operating frequency until the output meter again reads 50 mw (0.4 volt across 3.2 ohms) and note the frequency. Then tune it below the operating frequency until the same reference output reading is obtained and note the frequency. These are the 6 db attenuation points, or the bandwidth of the receiver.

Now advance the signal-generator output to 100 times the original level (40 db) and tune the signal generator above and below the receiver operating frequency until the output reference level is the same as before. Note the frequencies. These are the 40-db attenuation points.

SQUELCH

Most CB receivers now incorporate a squelch circuit. This circuit silences the speaker until a radio signal of a certain level is received. This threshhold is usually adjustable. The squelch is, in a sense, a sensitivity limiting device, and makes the receiver more selective in terms of signal strength. Some circuits are controlled by signal level (AVC voltage), others

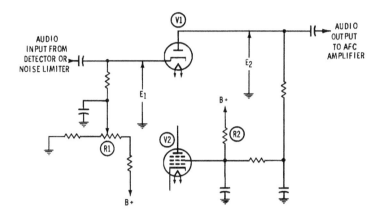

Fig. 5-22. Biased gate squelch circuit.

by reduction in background noise due to presence of a signal.

In the squelch circuit shown in Fig. 5-22, diode V1 is normally biased so that it cannot conduct and pass audio from the detector to the AF amplifier. E1 is greater than E2. Its plate is normally less positive than its cathode, which is biased positive at a value determined by the setting of squelch control R1. The plate voltage is obtained from the screen grid of an AVC controlled RF- or IF-amplifier tube (V2). When no signal, or a very weak signal, is received the screen voltage is low since the screen draws maximum current because of low AVC voltage. But, when a signal is received, the AVC voltage rises causing the screen of V2 to draw less current. The drop in R2 thus becomes smaller and the voltage (E2) applied to the plate of V1 rises. When E2 rises above E1, diode V2 conducts and the audio signal gets through.

Squelch Sensitivity

The level of signal required for E2 to rise above E1 (unsquelched) is the squelch sensitivity, and is determined by the setting of R1. To measure squelch sensitivity, set squelch control R1 just beyond the point that the background noise is silenced. Then feed a signal into the receiver input (as in Fig. 5-21) and adjust the input level to the point that the squelch "trips" and the modulated signal is heard. Note the signal level (microvolts). This is the squelch sensitivity.

102

Chapter 6

Power Sources

The electrical power requirements of a CB unit are many times greater than either the RF output when transmitting or the AF output when receiving. A typical CB set consumes 50 watts when delivering less than 4 watts RF output, and about 45 watts when delivering 2 watts of audio into a speaker. Tube-type sets are less efficient than transistor-type sets in terms of power consumed to power delivered.

In a tube-type set, the DC input voltage is converted into AC which is stepped up in potential and then converted back into DC. Tube filaments are sometimes energized directly from the DC-input power source, or sometimes by AC from a winding on the power transformer. Some transistor-type sets operate directly from the DC-input source. Hence, efficiency is higher, since there are fewer power conversion losses. Furthermore, transistors are often more efficient than tubes.

VEHICLE POWER SOURCE

The power source in a mobile installation is the engine which drives the generator. When the engine is running, the generator delivers electrical power. The battery is used as the power source only when the engine is not running, or when the load current is greater than the generator output current. On boats, the starting battery is often the CB-set power source.

Battery Voltage

The voltage across the terminals of the vehicle battery varies widely from its 12-volt level. When fully charged, it is usually 12.6 volts but even this is so only within a certain temperature range. On a cold day with the engine off, the battery voltage may be less than 12 volts. Depending on the voltage-regulator setting, with the engine running and the generator charging, battery voltage may rise as high as 15 volts. Therefore CB equipment must be designed to operate with input-voltage variations ranging from minus 10% to plus 25% of nominal. However, the performance is not the same at all input voltage levels—receiver sensitivity falls off and transmitter power-output drops when battery voltage is lower than normal, and vice versa. Excessively high maximum battery voltage can shorten the life of CB set components, tubes, and vibrators. It can sometimes cause transmitter power to rise above the 5-watt legal maximum input level or the 3.5-watt maximum permitted output level.

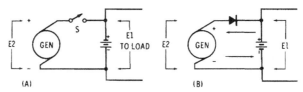

Fig. 6-1. Battery charging principles.

Battery Charging

In order to charge the battery, it is necessary to apply a charging voltage across it which is higher than the battery voltage. When switch S in Fig. 6-1A is open, battery voltage E1 is lower than generator voltage E2. When *S* is closed, E1 rises to the same level as E2 and current flows through the battery in an opposite-to-normal direction. The switch can be replaced by a diode, as shown in Fig. 6-1B. The diode allows charging current to flow when E2 is greater than E1, but it prevents current flow when the generator is not running or when E2 is smaller than E1.

The battery system of an auto usually consists of a 12-volt lead-acid storage battery, a DC generator driven by the vehicle engine, and a regulator. The regulator automatically connects the generator to the battery when the engine is running and the generator voltage is higher than the battery voltage. It also prevents generator voltage from rising above a preset, safe level at high engine speeds, and limits current flow to prevent damaging the battery or the generator.

Alternator

Alternators are now used in many cars in lieu of a DC generator. A typical system is shown in Fig. 6-2. The alternator produces three-phase AC, whose frequency varies with

104

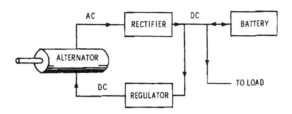

Fig. 6-2. Alternator charging system.

engine speed, which is converted into DC by a solid-state rectifier system. While the alternator and rectifier are of modern design, having no high-current moving contacts, regulators used with them still employ the traditional vibrating contacts. It is expected that transistors will be used in the near future to replace vibrating contacts in regulators.

Regulator

The level to which battery voltage rises with the engine running is determined by the regulator. Adjustments can be made to the regulator to set the maximum voltage level. This adjustment should be made only by an auto mechanic who has had the required training and experience, and should not be attempted by a radio specialist.

The battery voltage can be checked by the radio specialist to determine if regulator adjustment or replacement is required. The voltage can be measured by simply connecting a DC voltmeter across the battery terminals and noting the voltage with the engine turned off as well as with the engine running.

Measuring Battery Voltage Variations

A much more meaningful measurement can be made by using the meter expander circuit shown in Fig. 6-3. In this device, a 12-volt transistor dry battery is connected in series with the voltmeter. The dry battery polarity is in opposition to the storage battery polarity, as shown in the diagram. The meter measures the difference in potential of the two batteries. If the storage-battery potential (E1) is 12 volts and the dry-battery potential (E2) is also 12 volts, the difference in potential (E3) is zero. Hence, the meter will indicate zero.

When E1 is 12.6 volts and E2 is 12 volts, the meter reading (E3) will be 0.6 volts. With the engine running, if E1 rises to 14.4 volts, the meter will read 2.4 volts. If the DC volt-

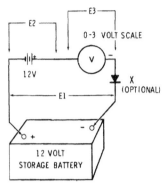

**Fig. 6-3. Methods for checking
variations in battery voltage.**

meter is set to its 0-3-volt scale, the change in battery voltage
from engine-off condition to engine-running at various speeds
can be read more accurately than when trying to read the
same changes on the 0-30-volt scale of a conventional meter.

It should be noted that the potential across the dry battery
is not always 12 volts. It may be slightly higher or lower,
depending on the condition of the battery. But the range of
difference potential is nevertheless more easily read using the
meter expander circuit. Diode X, shown in the diagram, can
be omitted; its sole purpose is to prevent damage to the meter
in the case of accidental reversal of the polarity of either
battery when making the test connections.

AC POWER SOURCES

Except in rare instances, 60-cycle AC electrical power is
available almost everywhere in the United States. In some
areas, the power frequency is 50 cycles. For some industrial
purposes, 25-cycle power is used. There are still areas in some
cities, and in some hotels and hospitals, where DC power
is used.

The AC line voltage is nominally 115 volts, but it may be
higher or lower. For this reason, much electrical equipment
is designed to operate safely when line voltage is anywhere
in the 105-130-volt range. A CB set operated at 105 volts
input may not perform satisfactorily. When operated at 130
volts input, the FCC input-power limit may be exceeded, and
tube and component life may be impaired. Where line voltage
is either excessively low or excessively high, a voltage adjusting transformer, such as the Acme type T10306 or Ohmite
type VT2F, can be used to provide the desired 115 volts.

Voltage Regulators

Where the line voltage varies widely, an automatic voltage regulator, such as Sola type 23-13-060 or Raytheon type RVA-60, can be used between the CB set and the power line. Both of these regulators are rated at 60 volt-amperes capacity, which is generally adequate. If the CB set consumes more power, a higher capacity regulator is required.

50-Cycle Power

Before operating a CB set on 50-cycle power, check the specification sheet or consult the manufacturer to determine whether the set can be operated safely at the lower power-line frequency—never attempt to operate a 60-cycle set from 25-cycle power.

CB POWER SUPPLIES

CB sets are available with integral power converters which enable direct operation of the set in one of the following combinations: 6 volts DC only, 12 volts DC only, 115 volts AC only, 6/12 volts DC, 6 volts DC/115 volts AC, 12 volts DC/115 volts AC, and 6/12 volts DC/115 volts AC. Sets designed for operation from 115 volts AC only can be operated from either a 6- or 12-volt DC source by the addition of an adaptor.

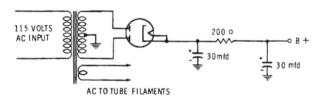

(A) Full-wave tube-type rectifier circuit.

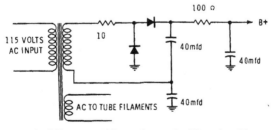

(B) Silicon rectifier voltage doubler circuit.
Fig. 6-4. AC power supplies.

AC Power Supplies

In a basic 115-volt AC power-supply circuit, the AC voltage fed into the primary of the power transformer is stepped down by one secondary to 6.3 volts or 12.6 volts AC for operation of tube filaments. The 115 VAC is stepped up by another secondary winding to obtain high voltage AC, which is rectified, filtered, and applied to the plates and screens of the tubes.

In this circuit a vacuum-tube rectifier is used. Silicon diodes are used in many sets instead of a rectifier tube. A full-wave, vacuum-tube rectifier is shown in Fig. 6-4A, and a silicon-rectifier voltage doubler is shown in Fig. 6-4B.

DC Power Supplies

DC input voltage must first be converted into AC in order to obtain high DC voltages. A DC power-supply block diagram is shown in Fig. 6-5. The DC-to-AC inverter may be a vibrator (Fig. 6-6A) or a pair of transistors (Fig. 6-6B).

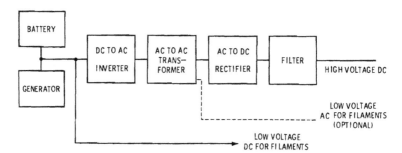

Fig. 6-5. Block diagram of DC power supply.

Vibrators—The vibrator is similar to a buzzer or doorbell. It is a high-speed electromechanical chopper or switch which alternately allows current to flow through one half of the power transformer primary and then the other half. This causes the direction of current flow to reverse alternately.

The flow of current, and the cessation of current flow in each half of the primary causes a magnetic field to envelope the secondary winding(s) which alternately reverses in direction. Hence, an AC voltage appears across the secondary winding(s). This AC voltage is not a true sine wave as is the case in an AC power supply. The transient impulses caused by the abrupt switching of the primary are erased by buffer

108

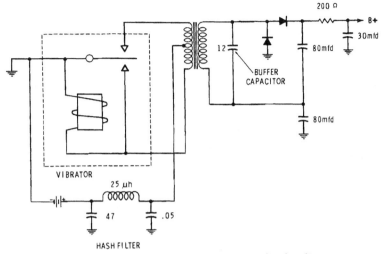

(A) Karr vibrator-type power supply circuit.

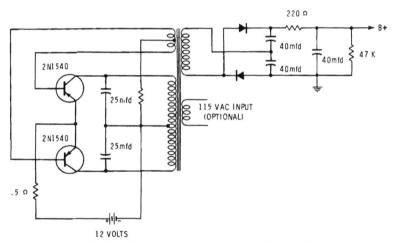

(B) Vocaline transistor power supply circuit.

Fig. 6-6. DC power supplies.

capacitor C, which also tends to smooth out the AC waveform.

Switching Transistors—Transistors are often used in lieu of a vibrator to switch primary current. They are used in an oscillator circuit in which one transistor conducts while the other is cut off, and vice versa. In effect, the transistors act as switches, but they have no moving contacts.

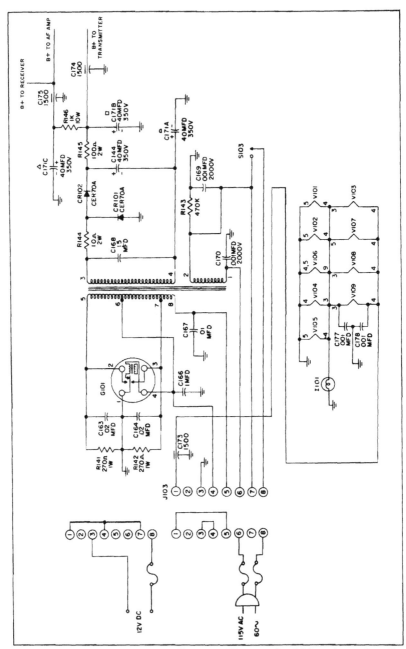

Courtesy Hammarlund Manufacturing Co.

Fig. 6-7. 12-volt DC/115-volt AC power supply.

Vibrators versus Transistors—Vibrators are widely used be-cause they cost less than power switching transistors. A plug-in vibrator can be replaced quickly, whereas power transistors are generally soldered into the circuit.

Transistor power supplies generally operate at a much higher frequency than vibrators, whose speed is limited by mechanical considerations. Because of the higher frequency, a smaller and lighter power transformer will suffice, and ripple filtering is easier; but the transformer design is more complex and thus more costly. Furthermore, the transistors must have heat-sinks and adequate ventilation.

Rectifiers and Filters—The same types of rectifiers and filters are used in power supplies that operate from DC or AC. They do not differ greatly among DC-only or AC-only power supplies. When operating from DC, special design pre-cautions may have to be taken to eliminate vibrator hash which is not present when operating from AC.

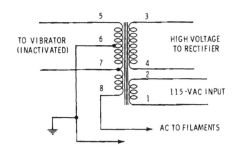

(A) When AC operated, AC is supplied to filaments.

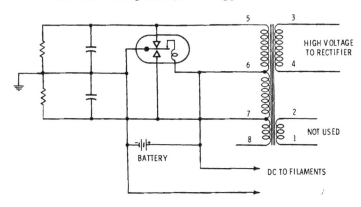

(B) When DC operated, filaments are supplied by the battery.
Fig. 6-8. AC/DC power supplies.

111

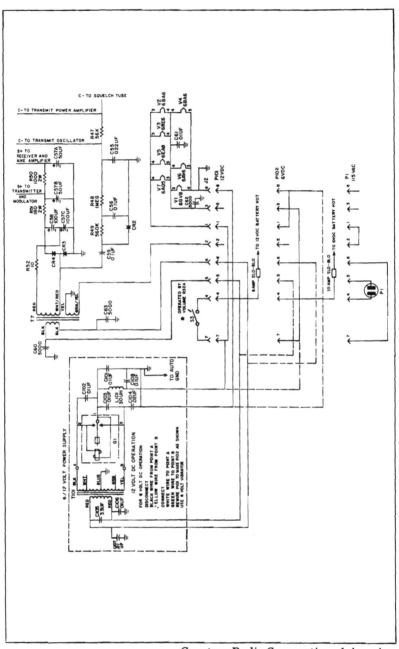

Fig. 6-9. AC power supply with DC adaptor—in dotted area.

AC/DC Power Supplies

The power-supply circuit shown in Fig. 6-7 is designed to permit operation from either 12 volts DC or 115 volts AC. The power transformer has two primary windings, 1-2 for AC input and 5-6-7 for DC input. When operated from AC, filament voltage is obtained from terminals 6-8 of the transformer, as shown in Fig. 6-8A. When operated from DC, filament voltage is obtained directly from the battery, as shown in Fig. 6-8B.

The change from DC operation to AC operation is made by using a different power cable whose connector bridges the circuits, as shown in Fig. 6-6.

DC Power Adaptors

Some CB sets with integral AC power supplies can be operated from DC by adding an inboard or outboard power converter. The internal power supply, whose circuit is shown in Fig. 6-9 requires 115 volts AC at the primary terminals (BLK-BLK) of the power transformer. This is normally obtained from a 115-volt AC power line. For DC operation, a 6- or 12-volt DC power supply is added, to convert the low DC voltage to 115 volts AC.

The DC power-supply adaptor can be operated from 12 volts DC, when wired as in Fig. 6-10A or from 6 volts DC when wired as in Fig. 6-10B. The vibrator must be replaced with one of appropriate voltage rating when changing from one DC input voltage to another.

The DC power supplies shown in Fig. 6-10 differ from conventional vibrator power supplies in that they do not employ a rectifier to reconvert the AC output voltage to DC.

DC-to-AC Power Inverters

CB sets equipped with AC power supplies are sometimes operated from DC through an external DC-to-AC inverter. There are many types of DC-to-AC inverters on the market; some employ vibrators and others employ switching transistors. When selecting an inverter, it is important to choose one that is capable of delivering adequate power on a continuous basis to avoid overheating and change in AC output voltage when switching the CB set from receive to transmit.

Nonstandard DC Voltages

CB sets are often used on materials handling vehicles for

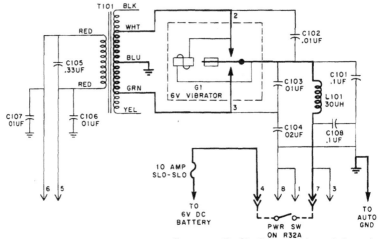

Courtesy Radio Corporation of America.

(A) Wired for 6-volt DC operation.

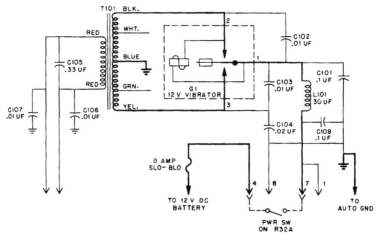

Courtesy Radio Corporation of America.

(B) Wired for 12-volt DC operation.

Fig. 6-10. 6/12-volt DC to AC power supply adaptors.

intraplant communications which are equipped with 24- or 36-volt storage batteries. When the set draws the same current when receiving or transmitting, the arrangement shown in Fig. 6-11 is sometimes used. The voltage is dropped by resistor R, which must have the correct resistance to drop the voltage from 24 or 36 volts to 12 volts with the CB set turned on. It must also be of sufficient power rating to handle the current safely.

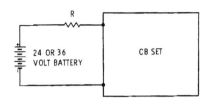

Fig. 6-11. Operating 12-volt set from higher DC voltage source.

For example, if the set draws 6 amperes at 12 volts, and the battery voltage is 24 volts, the resistor must have a value of 2 ohms, since R = E/I or 12/6 = 2. The resistor will consume 72 watts, since W = EI or 12 × 6 = 72 watts. Hence, a 100-watt or larger, resistor, is required to allow a margin of safety.

If the battery voltage is 36 volts, the resistor must cause a drop of 24 volts, and it must have a value of 4 ohms, since R = E/I or 24/6 = 4. The resistor will consume 144 watts since W = EI or 24 × 6 = 144. Hence, a 150-watt (or 200-watt), 4-ohm resistor should be used.

MOTOR-GENERATORS

The dropping resistor scheme will work satisfactorily only if the current used during transmit and receive are the same. When they are not the same, a more sophisticated arrangement is required. Usually, a motor-generator, or dynamotor, is used. A dynamotor converts DC at one voltage level to DC at another voltage level. It has a single armature with two windings, two commutators, and one field winding. A motor-generator, on the other hand, consists of a motor and a generator which may be two mechanically coupled machines, as shown in Fig. 6-2, or they may be combined as one machine.

To operate an AC-type CB set from a 24- or 36-volt DC source, a DC-to-AC motor-generator (motor-alternator), or rotary converter (inverter), may be used. The machine must be designed for continuous operation from the appropriate DC voltage and deliver 115 volts AC at 60 cps. However, when a DC-to-AC motor generator, or rotary converter, or an engine-driven AC generator is used as the power source, the AC voltage and frequency are apt to vary. Hence, the machine should be of the regulated type whose output frequency is 60 cps ± 3 cps and whose output voltage is held automatically to the 110-120-volt range.

Machine Noise

When a DC-to-DC or DC-to-AC rotating machine is used,

115

Fig. 6-12. Coaxial capacitors reduce motor-generator radio interference.

noise interference to CB reception might be caused by sparking between brushes and commutator and at voltage and speed regulator contacts. This interference can be minimized or eliminated by adding appropriate filters. In some cases, standard line filters, such as those made by Cornell-Dubilier, Aerovox, and Sprague, will do the trick. However, most standard line filters are designed to suppress interference at lower than CB frequencies and may not be sufficiently effective at 27 mc. Experimentation may be required to get rid of the noise. Coaxial capacitors, connected as shown in Fig. 6-12, might do the trick. Try various sizes of capacitors, grounding the outer sides of the capacitors to the machine frame. If these remedies are ineffective, consult the manufacturer of the machine who undoubtedly has had experience with radio interference problems.

AC POWER-SUPPLY TROUBLESHOOTING

An AC power supply generally delivers high-voltage DC at one or more levels between 150 and 260 volts, and low voltage AC at 6.3 or 12.6 volts for tube filaments.

While not listed in Chapter 2 as an essential servicing tool, an AC wattmeter can be a time saver when servicing AC-type

Fig. 6-13. Power input tester.

CB sets. Fig. 6-13 is a schematic of a simple input-power measuring device. The CB set is plugged into receptacle J and line plug P is plugged into an AC outlet. The wattmeter may be a Simpson model 79 with a range 0-75 watts, or a Triplett model 361 with a range of 0-150 watts.

When switch S is turned on and the CB set is turned on, the wattmeter indicates the amount of power consumed by the set. When first turned on, the reading may vary as tube filament resistance drops as the tubes warm up and plate current starts to flow. After the tubes have warmed up, the meter reading should stabilize and should be approximately the same as the power input specified in the instruction book. When the CB set is switched from receive to transmit, the meter reading may rise if the receive and transmit input-power requirements are not the same.

When an abnormally high-power input reading is obtained the moment the set is turned on, it indicates that there is a short circuit or excessive leakage in the set. If the set employs a tube rectifier in the power supply, pull the tube out of its socket and note the wattmeter reading. If it remains the same (too high), the trouble is probably a short either in the power transformer, the capacitor across the transformer high-voltage secondary (if there is one), or in the filament wiring. On the other hand, a large drop in input-power reading as the rectifier is removed indicates that the tube is shorted. However, after the rectifier tube is warmed up and its removal causes a large drop in input power, then the trouble is probably a shorted filter or bypass capacitor. If the set employs wired-in silicon rectifiers, this kind of trouble is indicated by excessively high input power the moment the set is turned on. Therefore, be ready to turn the set off at once.

When set to receive, an abnormally low power-input reading, after allowing the unit to warm up, indicates an open circuit (open silicon rectifier, resistor, or connection) or burned-out AF power-output tube or output-transformer primary. If power input is normal on receive and too low on transmit, look for a defective RF power-amplifier tube, open connection, etc.

Variations in power-input reading, after the set has warmed up and is in the receive position, indicate erratic conditions such as a leaky capacitor, defective resistor or intermittent tube. If the variations are noted only in the transmit position, look for defective components in the circuits that are activated only when transmitting. These could include the transmit crystal. Improper transmitter tuning could also cause unstable conditions which cause power input variations.

A wattmeter will quickly warn you of a dangerous short circuit condition (excessive power input). A very low-power reading most often indicates that the rectifier circuit is open. Improper operation, but with normal input-power indication, points out that the trouble is of a more subtle nature and is likely to require considerable intense investigation before it is found.

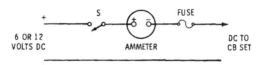

Fig. 6-14. Input current measurement.

DC Power Supply Current

A DC ammeter can be used for the same purpose as the wattmeter for checking sets operated from DC when connected as shown in Fig. 6-14. Be sure to observe meter and battery polarity, and use a quick-blow fuse (less than 10-amp rating for 12-volt sets, less than 20-amp for 6-volt sets) in the circuit to protect the meter.

When the set is first turned on, the meter reading may be quite high initially due to filament inrush current. If this current remains appreciably higher than the rated current, (consult the manufacturer's instruction book), turn off the set and look for a short-circuit condition. A stuck vibrator (or shorted transistor) could be the cause. After the tubes have warmed up, current should be approximately the same as specified in the instruction book. If it is too high, look for shorts and leakage. If it is too low, look for open circuits and a burned-out tube.

Variations in current, when the CB unit is set either to transmit or receive, could be due to a faulty vibrator or erratic buffer capacitor. If current variations are noted only in the transmit condition, look for trouble in the transmitter circuitry.

Physical Observations

When a wattmeter (AC sets) or ammeter (DC sets) is not available, power-supply troubles can sometimes be sensed by smell and sight. An odor about the power transformer may be present due to a stuck vibrator, a short in the transformer, buffer capacitor, rectifier, or in the circuitry beyond the rectifier. Chemical oozing from the transformer may also be present for the same reasons. A charred resistor is usually an indication of a short circuit or excessive leakage at the load side of the resistor.

Hum

Excessive hum, as heard in the speaker, is often due to an open or dehydrated filter capacitor or sometimes a shorted or leaky tube. Try a new filter capacitor of adequate voltage rating across each filter capacitor (observe capacitor polarity), one at a time, and note any change in hum level. To avoid damaging the rectifiers, start at the load end of the filter resistor (or choke) so that the capacitor will be charged before it is connected directly to the output of the rectifiers.

Hum can also be caused by a "tired" vibrator. In a set with transistors in the power supply, transistors may be switching at too low a frequency due to a defect in the power transformer or associated oscillator circuit capacitors or resistors.

Fuses

If the CB set fuse blows (if there is a fuse) when the set is first turned on, look for a stuck vibrator or short circuit. Make sure the fuse is of adequate rating, but not too high, to avoid damaging the set.

If the fuse blows after the set has been turned on for a time, the fuse may be of too low a value, or there may be a short condition or excessive leakage which develops after the set has warmed up.

REPLACING COMPONENTS

It is always best to replace such components as power transformers, vibrators and transistors with identical components. This is not always possible, particularly if the set is no longer on the market or if its manufacturer has gone out of business.

When transistors are used in the power supply, the power transformer is designed to work with the particular type of transistors used. The load characteristics also have an effect on transistor switching speed. If it is necessary to replace the power transformer, it may be wise to have it rewound if an exact replacement is not available.

Standard capacitors, resistors, and rectifiers of the same rating as the original, regardless of make, can normally be used to replace defective components.

Whenever replacing a vibrator or switching transistor, it is a good idea also to replace the buffer capacitor, using one of the same capacity and of the same or higher voltage rating.

PREVENTIVE MAINTENANCE

Vibrators have limited life and, as a preventive measure, should be replaced at regular intervals whose duration depends on the number of hours of use. When a set is turned on and off frequently, total vibrator life may be reduced and replacement after fewer hours of use may be required.

Transistors, on the other hand, may have extremely long life and may not require replacement for several years. Transistor life depends on the design of the set, input-voltage variations, ambient temperatures, and the manner in which the set is installed. Adequate transmission of heat away from the transistors is required. A heat sink in the set does this partially, although the heat sink must have a flow of air across it. The set should be installed away from other sources of heat and where there is adequate air circulation.

Chapter 7

Field Servicing

Troubles within a CB set are most easily corrected in the shop where adequate tools and test equipment are available. However, there are some troubles that are not caused by defects in the CB set and which must be corrected in the field.

Field servicing includes service calls at the customer's base stations, servicing of mobile units at locations away from the shop, and servicing mobile units at the shop location.

Time and money can be saved by using mass production techniques to check out a fleet of mobile units at one time. Taxi fleet owners, for example, often arrange to have groups or all mobile units checked out at specific intervals. The cab drivers bring their cabs to the shop at a prearranged time, and technicians, each assigned to handle a specific chore (such as frequency check, etc.) tackle one cab after another. This technique, while more commonly used in servicing commercial FM mobile units, can be applied to check-out of CB-equipped fleets.

A mobile CB check-out consists of the following steps:

1. Visual inspection of antenna, power wiring, mounting bracket, microphone, and microphone cord,
2. Measurement of transmitter frequencies (without removing the set from the vehicle),
3. Antenna-efficiency and RF power-output check (with thru-line-type RF power meter),
4. Receiver performance check (using a frequency meter placed near vehicle as signal source) with engine off and with engine running (to determine effects of voltage variations and presence of ignition interference),
5. Replacement of antenna, coaxial cable, etc., if required,
6. Replacement of CB set with a spare unit if set needs shop repair.

The same techniques are applicable whether checking out

a single mobile installation or a fleet, at the shop parking area or at the customer's location.

ANTENNA TESTS

When a mobile CB set does not operate, or reception and transmission range is very short and it has been determined that the set is receiving electric power, check the antenna system. This can be done quickly with a minimum of tools and test equipment.

All that is needed is a 12-volt lamp connected to the hot battery terminal and the antenna whip, as shown in Fig. 7-1.

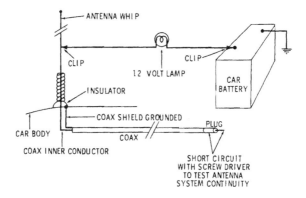

Fig. 7-1. Quick antenna check.

The lamp should light when the plug at the set end of the coaxial cable (pin and shell) is shorted with a screw driver. If it does not light, the coaxial cable is open, the plug is not properly connected, or the cable shield is not grounded at the antenna base.

On the other hand, if the lamp lights without shorting the coax plug, the cable is shorted, the antenna whip is grounded, or the cable shield is touching the center conductor at the plug pin. This is not true when the antenna is of the shunt-fed base-loaded type shown in Fig. 7-2, in which case the lamp should glow when the coax plug is shorted or not shorted.

It may be more convenient to listen to a buzzer or bell instead of trying to see if a lamp lights, particularly in daylight. An audible indicator can be used to test antenna circuits for continuity and shorts (Fig. 7-3). Disconnect the coax plug from the CB set and short the pin to the shell. The buzzer

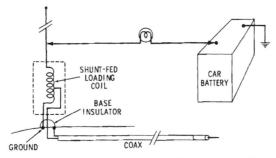

Fig. 7-2. Some types of antenna will indicate a short.

(or bell) should sound when the plug is shorted, and it should be silent when the plug is not shorted, except when the antenna is of a special type which normally has a DC shunt to ground.

The above go-no-go tests will reveal DC shorts and open circuits. When one of these defects occurs, the antenna will be ineffective. If the set worked properly before, such a defect can be the cause of nonoperation or drastic impairment of performance.

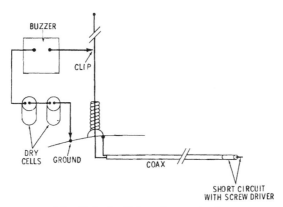

Fig. 7-3. Audible antenna check.

Field-Strength Meter Test

On the other hand, if the CB set never did perform properly after installation in the vehicle, a short or open in the antenna system could be the cause. Inadequate range can also be caused by failure of the antenna to load properly. A quick way to determine whether the antenna is capable of radiating

123

a signal at all is to place a field-strength meter a few feet from the antenna, as shown in Fig. 7-4. After listening to make sure the channel is not in use, turn the transmitter on (with antenna plug connected), announce the station call letters, and watch the needle of the field-strength meter. If it indicates zero, the antenna is not radiating.

Low-cost field-strength meters which consist of a crystal-detector diode and a meter and are suitable for this purpose are available from many sources (Lafayette, Heath, Allied, etc.).

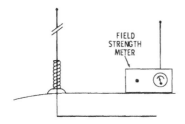

Fig. 7-4. Field strength test.

Antenna-Efficiency Test

A field-strength meter of this type is a handy go-no-go tester. To determine the efficiency of the antenna with greater precision, a thru-line RF-power meter can be used, connected in series with the antenna. There are many low-cost instruments of this type (available from Seco, Lafayette, Heath, Allied, etc.). Higher-priced instruments of this type are made by Bird and Sierra. They are sometimes called antenna checkers, reflected-power meters, bidirectional RF power meters, etc.

Fig. 7-5. Portable signal- and antenna-checking meter.

Such an instrument measures two conditions: *incidental,* or forward, power (power delivered by the transmitter) and *reflected,* or reverse, power (power reflected back and not absorbed by the antenna). The smaller the difference between these readings, the less efficient is the antenna. If the test reveals that a large percentage of the power is being reflected (not absorbed by the antenna), the trouble is usually due to improper tuning of the transmitter-output circuits, a defect in the antenna system, or improper antenna length or type. Fig. 7-5 shows an instrument of this type which can also be used as a field-strength meter.

Antenna-System Leakage

If the set performed properly in the past and performance deteriorated gradually, the trouble could be due to deterioration of the coaxial cable. Measure the leakage resistance of

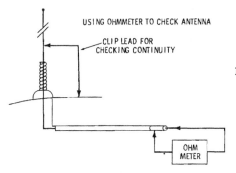

USING OHMMETER TO CHECK ANTENNA

CLIP LEAD FOR
CHECKING CONTINUITY

OHM
METER

Fig. 7-6. Antenna ohmmeter check.

the antenna system with an ohmmeter (Fig. 7-6). The meter should indicate an open circuit, unless the antenna contains a shunt-fed loading coil. The resistance measured with a megohmmeter should be in the order of hundreds of megohms— beyond the range of typical ohmmeters. If leakage is detected, clean the insulator at the antenna base. If this does not eliminate evidence of leakage, disconnect the coax from the antenna. A leakage indication, with the antenna disconnected, makes it evident that the coaxial cable is defective and should be replaced.

An ohmmeter can also be used for checking antenna-circuit continuity and proper grounding by connecting a clip lead (Fig. 7-6).

POWER-SOURCE TROUBLES

Lack of electric power is easy to detect. If the pilot lamp (if there is one) does not light or if the tubes do not light, power is not reaching the CB set. The trouble could be due to an open connection inside the set or in the external wiring, or a blown fuse.

A quick way to find out is to disconnect the CB set battery cable from the electrical system of the vehicle and measure the resistance across the CB unit battery leads with the set On-Off switch turned on. The resistance should be close to zero. If you get an open-circuit indication, check the cable, power plug, fuse, and power-circuit wiring of the set. Sometimes, electric power reaches the CB set, but the voltage at the set (with the set turned on) may be inadequate to operate the set. If the vehicle battery is fully charged, the trouble is usually due to a high-resistance connection. If this trouble is suspected, disconnect the set battery cable from the vehicle electrical system and temporarily connect the cable leads directly to the battery. Watch polarity—make sure the battery ground lead is not inadvertently connected to the hot battery terminal.

Should the results be the same with the CB unit battery cable connected directly to the battery, as when connected to the ammeter or other power take-off point, run the vehicle engine at fairly high speed. If the set operates satisfactorily under these conditions, the battery could be the cause of the trouble; or the vibrator may be tired and fails to start at normal engine-off voltage (in which case it should be replaced).

In some cases, the CB set may operate erratically or spill over into oscillation when the engine is running, if the voltage regulator is improperly adjusted. The voltage should not rise above 7.2 volts (6-volt battery) or 14.4 volts (12-volt battery). If it does, have the vehicle voltage regulator adjusted by a competent auto-electrician.

MOBILE FREQUENCY CHECKS

CB transmitter frequencies can be checked without removing the CB set from the vehicle, if a portable, battery-operated frequency meter is available. The techniques are the same as described in Chapter 3. In extremely cold or hot weather the frequency measurements may be inaccurate if the frequency meter is not temperature-controlled. (The transmitter frequency may also vary under such climatic extremes.)

When making transmitter-frequency measurements with the CB set connected to a radiating antenna, listen to make sure the channel is clear before turning the transmitter on. Keep test transmissions short, and be sure to announce the station call letters. If the channel is too busy to make such measurements without causing interference to others, disconnect the antenna and connect the CB set antenna terminal to a dummy load.

RECEIVER PERFORMANCE CHECKOUT

When other stations can be heard, it is easy to determine if the receiver is sensitive by merely listening. In the absence of such signals, you can use a frequency meter if it contains a tone modulator as a signal source. Connect a short piece of wire or plug-in whip antenna to the frequency meter and place the instrument at a reasonable distance from the mobile unit. With the CB-set squelch control set to the fully *unsquelched* position, turn the frequency meter on and off and note if the signal quiets the receiver background noise.

Make these tests with the vehicle engine off and with the engine running, noting changes in performance. If the CB set has a noise limiter, turn the noise limiter on and off. When turned on, popping noises should be diminished in level and the test-signal audio level may also drop slightly.

EXCESSIVE NOISE

The most common complaint about mobile CB installations is noise. Rushing background noise indicates that the receiver is sensitive, but the signals are not strong enough. This condition is usually due to a defect in the antenna system. Sometimes it is due to the fact that the signals being heard are coming in from a great distance and are not strong enough to override residual receiver noise.

Popping noises heard when the vehicle engine is not running are usually picked up from other vehicles in the vicinity. Popping noises heard when the vehicle engine is running, and varying in rate as the engine speed is changed, are caused by the ignition system. A whining sound, heard only when the engine is running is usually caused by the generator.

Many cars are factory-equipped with ignition- and generator-noise suppressors. Instead of conventional spark-plug and distributor suppressors (series resistors), wire possessing several thousand ohms of resistance per foot is often used as sparkplug- and distributor-to-ignition-coil leads. A capacitor is generally connected across the generator armature terminal and the generator frame. Another capacitor is connected across body ground and the "hot" battery lead, generally at the ignition switch or ammeter.

This type of noise suppression is nearly always adequate for standard AM broadcast reception, and sometimes for CB reception. In some cases, more adequate noise suppression is required for CB reception, since ignition noise is of greater intensity at 27 mc than at lower frequencies.

Various types of noise-suppression kits, designed especially for CB radio, are available. Hallett Manufacturing Company, 5910 Bowcroft St., Los Angeles 16, Calif. manufactures an ignition noise suppression kit which includes shielded ignition cables, shields for the ignition coil and voltage regulator as well as spark plug shields. Sprague Products Company, North Adams, Mass. offers a noise suppression kit (*Suppresskit* Type SK-1) which is designed specifically for CB use. Considerable work has been done in the field of radio interference suppression by the Belden Manufacturing Co., P.O. Box 5070A, Chicago 80, Illinois. This company has developed a special cable (IRS Cable) for use in auto ignition systems, and has printed small folders dealing with suppression problems, e.g., *Technical Data-Automotive* Section #5, and #6.

Also available is a booklet entitled *Giving Two-Way Radio Its Voice*, from the Automotive Technical Services Department, Champion Spark Plug Co., Toledo 1, Ohio.

The location of the antenna may contribute to noise pick up. Generally, it should be as far from the engine as possible. Care should be exercised in routing the coax away from wiring which may act as carriers for ignition noise.

Many late-model cars are now equipped with rectifier-alternators in lieu of a DC generator. Since a commutator is not used, the whining generator noise is eliminated. However, there have been cases where the built-in silicon rectifiers combined with the alternator frame to produce radio signals at frequencies that cause interference.

BASE-STATION SERVICING

While a CB set is small enough to be brought into the shop for servicing, there may be troubles in the antenna system or power source, as well as troubles that exist because of the base-station environment, which require the attention of a technician at the base-station site.

Base-Station Antenna Troubles

The antenna at a base station may be inaccessible for inspection without taking it down. The system (antenna and transmission line) can be checked for short circuits and leakage by connecting an ohmmeter across the coax plug at the set end of the cable, as shown in Fig. 7-6 (should indicate open circuit). A cable continuity test cannot be made, as shown in the diagram, unless the antenna is accessible, in which case the clip lead should be connected across the radiating element and the ground plane; a short-circuit condition should be indicated, but only when the test clip lead is in place. The above tests are not applicable when the antenna has a matching arrangement which provides a DC path across the antenna.

The most meaningful test of any type of CB antenna is made with a thru-line-type RF power meter, connected in the same manner as at mobile stations (Fig. 7-5).

Base-Station Receiver Check-Out

A quick way to determine if the antenna system is the cause of unsatisfactory reception is to try a plug-in antenna in place of the outside antenna. While seldom as satisfactory as an outside antenna, better performance with an indoor antenna indicates that the outdoor antenna system is at fault. This may not be the case when the outdoor coaxial cable is excessively long.

Listening to other CB signals is the quickest way to determine if the receiver is operating in a reasonably satisfactory manner. When there are no signals from other stations, use a frequency meter as a signal source, explained earlier.

Base-Station Power

The base-station electric power source is usually 60-cycle AC at approximately 115 volts. Most sets will operate satisfactorily when line voltage is as low as 110 volts. At lower input voltages, instability of the receiver local oscillator and transmitter oscillator may occur.

The availability of power can be easily determined by temporarily connecting a lamp to the AC outlet. If there is power at the outlet, there should be power at the CB set, when its power cord is plugged into the outlet. If not, the set's fuse may be blown or there may be an open connection. Look particularly for a broken connection at the molded AC plug at the end of the cord. If this is the case, or it is strongly suspected that it is, snip the cord an inch or so from the plug and install a new plug with screw terminals.

If the unit power plug fits loosely into the AC outlet, or it is necessary to bend the plug blades to make contact, try another AC outlet and advise the customer to have the power receptacle (convenience outlet) replaced. Poor connections here are a source of noise and erratic operation.

Grounding the Set

Under some conditions, the CB set cabinet (if metal) is "hot" with respect to ground. The user may get a shock when touching the set while standing on a concrete or metal floor, or when also touching a grounded object. The metal case of a microphone could, under some circumstances, be dangerous to touch.

This potential shock hazard can be avoided by grounding the chassis of the CB set. The reasons for the existence of this shock hazard are illustrated in Fig. 7-7. One side of the AC

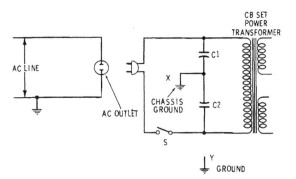

Fig. 7-7. CB unit AC input circuit.

power line is normally grounded; the other side of the power line is therefore hot with respect to ground. The typical CB set contains a line filter consisting of two capacitors, C1 and C2, one connected to each side of the power line and chassis ground. They are, in effect, in series with each other, across the AC line. Their midpoint, which is connected to the chassis ground, is the midpoint of the voltage divider which they form. Hence, with the power switch (S) of the set turned on, the chassis is at a potential of approximately 57 volts above ground. With the power switch open, and the set power plug

130

connected to the line, as shown in the diagram, the chassis is at a potential approximately 115 volts above ground. By reversing the plug in the AC outlet, the chassis will be at ground potential with the power switch turned off, and at half the line voltage above ground with the switch on.

When the set chassis is at a potential above ground, as described earlier, the current that can flow between the set chassis and ground is limited by the reactance of the capacitors (270,000 ohms for 0.01 ufd capacitor, 27,000 ohms for 0.1 ufd capacitor, at 60 cps).

By grounding the CB set chassis, the shock hazard is avoided, since point X (chassis) and point Y (external ground) in Fig. 7-7 are now at the same potential. The voltage across C1 is now the full AC line voltage and the voltage across C2 is zero. If the power plug is reversed in the AC outlet, the reverse is true.

The chassis of a CB set operated from house current is automatically grounded through the shield of the antenna transmission line (coaxial cable) if the antenna ground plane is grounded. If it is not, touching the antenna could cause a shock, unless the set chassis is grounded. The chassis ground connection sometimes reduces noise pick-up and hum. Mainly, it adds safety. Capacitors C1 and C2 help reduce noise transmission to the set through the power transformer.

To ground a CB set, securely connect a wire to the chassis (under a screw head, etc., if a ground terminal is not provided). Connect the other end of the wire to a cold water pipe, using a ground clamp. If the ground clamp makes an imperfect connection to the pipe, new troubles may be created. If a cold water pipe is not available, a radiator is a fair substitute. Avoid gas pipes.

Noisy Reception

Ignition interference from cars in the vicinity is the prime source of CB interference. It is difficult to control when the noise transmitters are autos owned by others. Some relief is obtained when the CB set contains a noise limiter. The real cure would be the enactment and enforcement of a law that would require all vehicles to be treated so as to prevent radiation of electrical interference.

At a base station, if the set does not have a built-in noise limiter, an outboard accessory noise limiter can be added. If the ignition interference is troublesome, even when a noise limiter is used, additional improvement in noise reduction can be made by moving the antenna farther away from the street and areas traversed by motor vehicles. This is often impractical. Ignition noise is one of the annoyances CB users must learn to live with, at least until more effective noise suppression means are developed.

Noise is also picked up from the house electrical wiring and electrical appliances. The causes and elimination of electrical interference is a subject in itself, well covered in other books on the subject.

Base-Station Transmitter Check-Out

Use a thru-line-type RF power meter to check out transmitter output and antenna efficiency as described earlier. Before turning the transmitter on, listen first to make sure the channel is clear. If the channel is busy, and you can't afford to wait until it is clear, use a lamp-type dummy antenna load to check the transmitter and note its brilliance with the transmitter turned on. When talking into the microphone, the brilliance of the lamp should flicker at a rate depending on the audio frequencies.

TWO-WAY COMMUNICATION CHECK-OUT

The proof of operational adequacy is the quality of the results achieved in actual use. If the customer has a mobile unit within range, try exchanging communications with it. If a customer's mobile unit is not available, you can talk to the CB set in your shop if it is within range and is equipped to operate on any of the customer's channels. Do not attempt to communicate with other CB stations operated by strangers, since this would be in violation of FCC rules. You can legally communicate from a customer's base station with your own shop base station only on those channels that are for interstation use. For this purpose, one of the 23-channel-type CB sets is a handy shop tool.

FIELD REPAIRS

Field repair of CB sets is usually limited to replacement of tubes and vibrators. Replacement of crystals and repairs which can affect transmitter performance (exclusive of tube replacement) should be made only in the shop where adequate transmitter performance checks can be made.

132

SPARE SETS

A business user of CB buys his equipment to serve his needs, and once having become accustomed to having two-way radio, he is likely not to be pleased if he has to stay off the air while his equipment is being repaired. A good way to please customers is to loan them a spare set while their equipment is being repaired.

Chapter 8

Shop Servicing

Adequate test equipment is required in the shop to make frequency measurements, measure performance, and diagnose troubles due to component failures. However, diagnosis of many troubles can be made with virtually no instruments, although AC power must be available for checking AC-operated sets, and a battery or rectifier for checking DC-operated sets.

Many CB set troubles can be diagnosed without having to dismantle the set. Only a few tools and a test lamp or two are required to find the cause of the majority of troubles in a hurry. The most essential device is a neon-lamp, line-voltage checker which can be bought in almost any hardware store for a dollar. No tools or testers are required for some tests.

CHECK ITS TEMPERATURE

The following check-out procedures can be made without taking the set apart, except to the extent required to get at the tubes.

With power connections made to a 6- or 12-volt battery or AC power line, depending on the set requirements, (on DC make sure polarity is correct) and the set power switch is turned on, the tubes should light. Look at them in a subdued light since the glow in some tubes may be difficult to see due to the coating on the inside of the glass. If the tubes light and there is no odor or smoke issuing from the set, leave it on for several minutes; and then, touch the tubes with your fingers—they should all feel warm to the touch. A cold or unlighted tube should be replaced with a new one of the same type. The set itself should feel warm to the touch after a few minutes of operation.

If all tubes fail to light, recheck the power connections and try a new fuse (if the set has one). If the tubes light but none get more than slightly warm, chances are that the trouble is in the power supply. The vibrator in a vibrator-powered, DC-operated set should hum when your ear is placed close to it. Try a new vibrator if there is no hum, or the tubes do not heat up appreciably.

When it has been determined that the set is receiving power, connect a shop test antenna to the receiver-antenna connector receptacle.

NO SOUND

With the transmit-receive switch set to Receive, and with the volume and squelch controls set wide open, a rushing noise should normally be heard in the speaker. If no sound is heard, not even a hum, pull out the audio power-amplifier tube (usually a 6AQ5 which also functions as the transmitter modulator) and listen for a "click" in the speaker. If unsure which tube to pull out of its socket, pull them all out, re-inserting each tube before pulling another. To avoid a possible burn, wear a glove or use a cloth when pulling tubes, some of them can get quite hot.

Speaker Check

If no click is heard, and the tubes light and are warm, the trouble may be either in the speaker circuit or the audio

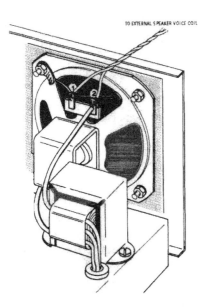

TO EXTERNAL SPEAKER VOICE COIL

Fig. 8-1. Speaker connections.

power-amplifier stage. Connect an external speaker (any size permanent-magnet type) through a pair of wires to the terminals of the CB set speaker (terminals 1 and 2, Fig. 8-1). If the set works now, replace the speaker.

When a spare speaker is not available, the set speaker can be checked (with the set turned off) by momentarily connecting the speaker terminals to a 1.5-volt flashlight cell. A click should be heard. If it is not heard, the speaker is defective.

Tube Substitution

On the other hand, if a click is heard when one or more tubes are pulled out of their sockets, the speaker circuit is apparently operative. In this case, try a new tube in each socket, one at a time, putting each old tube back into its socket if a new one doesn't cure the trouble. Allow enough time for the tube to warm up when trying a new one.

Crystal Substitution

In a fixed-tuned set which does not have a tuning dial, and which is equipped with crystals for only one channel, a defective crystal could make the receiver silent. Try a new receiver crystal, if one is available, even if it isn't for the right channel. If a new crystal brings back the background noise, the old crystal should be replaced. It is also possible that the local oscillator could be so badly mistuned that it won't oscillate with the correct crystal inserted. The crystal replacement must be one that is ground to the same frequency as the original in order to receive on the same channel.

When substitution of the receiver crystal, tubes, or vibrator does not restore proper operation, the trouble is probably of such a nature that the set must be dismantled and a more sophisticated diagnosis performed.

NOISE BUT NO RECEPTION

The existence of a background rushing noise generally indicates that the receiver is functioning, although it may not be tuned to the right frequency. If the receiver is of the fixed-tuned type and is equipped for only one channel, crystal trouble is indicated. If no signals are heard after the proper receiver crystal for the channel has been replaced, this may be only because there is no one on the air on that channel at that moment. Try a crystal ground for another channel.

The trouble could be in the antenna switching circuit (often part of the transmit-receive switch or relay). Try operating the push-to-talk switch several times; this might clean dirty contacts sufficiently to restore operation. If it does, examine the switch (or relay) contacts—cleaning them with contact cleaning fluid might be the cure.

It is possible, although not probable, that the IF transformer tuning has drifted sufficiently to make the receiver sensitive at an undesired frequency and inoperative at the desired frequency. In the case of a double-conversion superheterodyne receiver, this kind of trouble could be due to frequency drift of either the first or second local oscillator. Try new crystals in both oscillators. Retuning the self-excited oscillator, if the receiver has one, might restore proper reception. More elaborate measures, to be discussed later, are generally required.

NOISY RECEPTION

Noisy reception could be a normal condition, particularly if the noise is caused by the ignition systems of nearby cars and trucks.

The condition of reception accompanied by a steady rushing noise could also be normal, if the incoming CB signals are weak. When a strong signal is received, the background noise should subside.

Causes of noisy reception, poor contact at the antenna switch (or relay), defective vibrator-hash-suppression filters, or misalignment of the IF transformers, will require more elaborate means for detection.

INSENSITIVITY

Inadequate receiver sensitivity is often manifested by low background noise when a signal is not being intercepted. Receiver insensitivity is most often caused by a defective tube. A quick way to find out if tubes are the cause is to replace each tube, one at a time, waiting for the new tube to warm up and noting any improvement in performance.

Lack of sensitivity can also be due to poor contact in the antenna switching circuit, or misalignment of tuned circuits. Misalignment can occur gradually, due to aging of components which cause physical changes in the components, resulting in changes in their electrical characteristics until the set no longer responds properly to the desired signals.

POOR SELECTIVITY

Interference from adjacent channel stations is sometimes due to misalignment of the IF transformers or defective receiver crystals. Try a new receiver crystal. Often it is a normal condition—some sets are not as selective as others, and their tuned circuits are unable to reject unwanted strong adjacent-channel signals. Sometimes, of course, the offending station is not on its correct frequency.

ERRATIC PERFORMANCE

Sudden changes in the volume of an intercepted CB signal can be caused by poor connections, faulty tubes, and intermittent capacitors. Tap the tubes, one at a time, while listening to a station and note any change in performance or introduction of noise. Try a new tube if one is found that is affected by tapping. If performance is affected, or noise is introduced, when striking the set gently, look for loose connections. Pay special attention to connector plugs and receptacles.

NO TRANSMISSION

When the receiver operates but the set apparently won't transmit, place a field strength meter near the test antenna, and set the push-to-talk switch to transmit. If the meter indicates that power is being radiated, talk loudly into the microphone. The meter reading should vary as you talk. If not, try a new microphone. If the meter indicates that the transmitter is not operating, disconnect the antenna (with transmitter off) and connect a No. 47 pilot-lamp dummy load to the set antenna connector. The lamp should glow when the transmitter is on.

INADEQUATE TRANSMITTING RANGE

If the customer complains that transmitting range is shorter than normal, the trouble may be due to inadequate transmitter power output, insufficient modulation, or both. Transmitter power output and modulation can be checked quickly by connecting a No. 47 dummy load to the set antenna connector as described earlier. When the transmitter is turned on, the lamp should glow brightly. When talking loudly into the microphone, the lamp brilliance should increase in accordance with modulation changes.

Inadequate transmitter power can be caused by an inactive crystal. Try a new transmitter crystal and note any difference in lamp brilliance. (If you leave a new crystal in place, measure the transmitter frequency.) A weak tube can be the cause —try new ones and note any improvement. Check the receiver tuned circuits—the transmitter could require retuning.

Low modulation level can be caused by a weak tube, improperly tuned transmitter circuits, or a low-output microphone. Holding the microphone too far away or talking too softly can also be the cause of inadequate modulation. Maximum range and voice volume at distant receivers are obtained when the modulation level is high. If in doubt about modulation level, try a new microphone of the same type, or a different type microphone of the same impedance, and note if there is any greater increase in test-lamp brilliance.

Precautions

When a blown fuse is replaced and the new fuse blows, do not attempt to operate the set until the cause of the overload is found and corrected. If an odor or smoke is detected when the set is turned on, shut off the set and look for a scorched part. Continued operation may cause additional damage.

Make sure the battery polarity is correct (usually the red wire is positive, and the black wire is negative) before turning the set on. Some sets operate with either polarity; others, particularly those employing transistors instead of a vibrator in the power supply, might be damaged when input-power polarity is reversed.

Since electrical potentials as high as 300 volts can be encountered, exercise caution to avoid shocks when touching circuit elements and wiring when the set is turned on. When working on a set operated from AC power on the bench, securely ground the chassis or stand on a dry rubber mat.

Do not bend, file, or sandpaper switch or relay contacts. If they need cleaning, use a professional contact-burnishing tool or contact-cleaning fluid. To be safe, it may be wiser to replace a switch or relay with faulty contacts than to attempt to repair it.

Never make prolonged transmitter tests with the set connected to a radiating antenna, since you can cause harmful interference to others who may want to use the channel. Instead, use a dummy antenna, such as a No. 47 lamp.

When a transmitter connected to an antenna is tested, keep transmissions short and announce the call letters assigned to the transmitter (posted on license tag attached to set).

If a transmitter crystal is replaced, do not turn the trans-

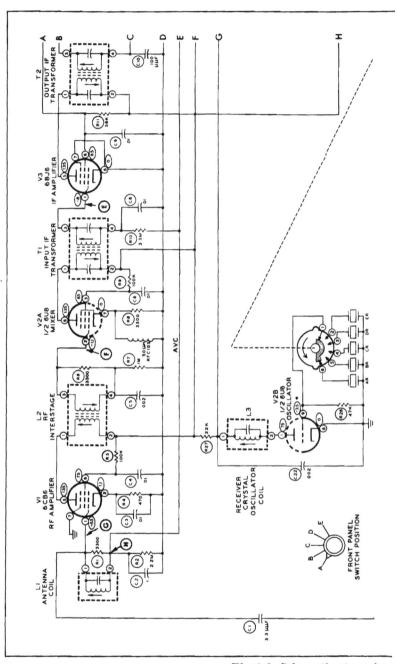

Fig. 8-2. Schematic of receiver

140

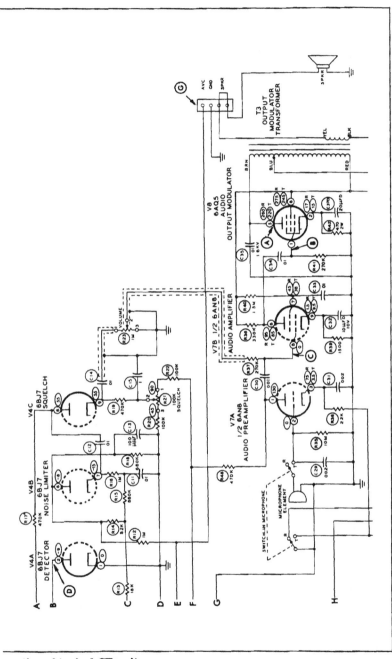

portion of typical CB unit.

mitter on when connected to an antenna until the transmitter frequency has been measured and found to be within tolerance. The transmitter cannot lawfully be put on the air after replacement of a transmitter crystal, or after any work has been done that can affect the frequency, until it has been checked out by, or under the supervision of, a properly licensed radio operator. The exception is when the transmitter oscillator is a sealed unit which can be replaced in its entirety.

Do not tamper with internal receiver or transmitter tuning adjustments, except when you have adequate test equipment available.

SERVICING WITH INSTRUMENTS

The place to start, when diagnosing CB set troubles, is at the beginning—the power input source. Use an ammeter (DC operation) or wattmeter (AC operation) in the power input circuit, as described in Chapter 6, to determine if the set is drawing rated, excessive or too little current or power. If the power used is either excessive or too little, it is immediately known that a short or open circuit condition exists within the set and the set must be disassembled.

Signal Tracing

If the set draws rated current or power, the receiver can be quickly checked by applying a signal to the antenna connector. Handy for quick checking is a probe-type oscillator which contains a multivibrator that produces essentially an all-frequency signal. Touch the probe of the tiny signal generator to the center contact of the antenna connector—a loud tone should be heard.

If no tone is heard (with volume and squelch controls wide open) expose the bottom of the set chassis and touch the signal generator probe to the plate terminal of the AF power-amplifier tube socket (point A in Fig. 8-2). If no tone is heard in the speaker, measure the DC plate voltage between point A and the chassis. If there is plate voltage, the trouble could be an open speaker, open output transformer secondary (not likely), or an open connection in the speaker-control portion of the transmit-receive switching circuit.

If the tone is heard, touch the probe to the grid terminal of the AF power amplifier tube (point B in Fig. 8-2). The tone heard in the speaker should be much louder. If no tone is heard, the tube could be defective or cathode resistor R42 open.

If the tone is heard, move the signal generator probe to the grid of the first audio amplifier (C), then to the plate of the detector (D), and successively to the grids of the IF amplifier (E), mixer (F) and RF amplifier (G). The tone should be heard in each instance.

However, if no tone is heard when the signal is injected at C, the trouble is either in the first audio-amplifier stage, or coupling capacitor C34. No tone at point D indicates trouble in the noise limiter or squelch circuits. Absence of tone when signal is injected at E or F indicates trouble between the test point and the preceding test point; somewhere in the IF amplifier circuits. If no tone is heard, or the tone is weak, when signal is injected at G, the trouble could be in the RF amplifier stage or in the local oscillator (V2B).

Using a Tunable Signal Generator

The preceding procedure is a simple way to localize the cause of inoperation of a receiver. If, instead of a multivibrator type of signal injector, a conventional tunable RF signal generator is used, it will be necessary to tune the signal generator to the appropriate frequency. In the case of the receiver shown in Fig. 8-2, a modulated signal at 455 kc can be injected at points D, E, and F, and at the receiver operating frequency (27-mc band) at points F and G. The ground (shield) of the signal-generator output lead is connected to the CB set chassis, and the hot lead is connected through a small capacitor (10 mmf or so) to the signal injection points.

If it is suspected that the local oscillator is not functioning, this can be verified by injecting an unmodulated signal at point F through a very small capacitor (2 mmf or so) slowly tuning the signal generator through the 26-28-mc range. With an antenna connected to the CB set, you should be able to tune in CB stations since the signal generator functions as a tunable local oscillator.

The same techniques can be used in diagnosing troubles in double-conversion and triple-conversion superheterodyne receivers, working from the audio amplifier back through the IF amplifier stages, the mixers, and the RF amplifier.

Voltage Tests

Receiver troubles can also be diagnosed by measuring DC voltages at the various tube sockets. The correct voltages are often noted on receiver schematics or in voltage measurement tables published in instruction books. However, there are instances when all DC voltages appear to be normal, yet the set will not operate because a signal path somewhere in the set is open.

There is one DC voltage, however, that depends on the RF signal; that is the AVC voltage. In the set whose diagram is shown in Fig. 8-2, an external terminal is provided for measuring AVC voltage (point G in the diagram). This terminal is not provided in most CB sets. In the absence of such a terminal, AVC voltage can be measured at point H (Fig. 8-2). AVC voltage should be measured with a DC VTVM instead of a VOM to avoid loading down the AVC bus by the lower meter resistance of the VOM.

When a signal is being received, or when a signal is injected at the antenna terminal or points G, F, or E, the AVC voltage should rise. If it does not rise, or there is no AVC voltage, the signal is not getting through as far as the detector.

Replacing Receiver Components

Capacitors in the RF-amplifier, mixer, and local-oscillator stages are apt to be critical and each should always be replaced by one of identical type, value, and rating, except for cathode, B+ feed, and screen-bypass capacitors. In some sets, these too may be critical.

All coils should be replaced by identical types. However, replacement of IF transformers with standard general replacement types may not be harmful. Sometimes, the selectivity characteristics of the receiver might be affected, or instability may result due to higher than normal gain. Be careful to dress leads as they were originally to avoid creation of unwanted feedback paths.

In general, replacement of tubes should create no problems.

TRANSMITTER DIAGNOSIS

CB transmitters are very simple. They generally consist of only an oscillator and an RF power amplifier (some have more stages), and utilize the receiver audio amplifier as the amplitude modulator. Some have an extra audio stage which is used only when transmitting, for example, V7A in Fig. 8-2.

Test Points

Some transmitters are equipped with an RF power meter to facilitate tuning without requiring external test equipment.

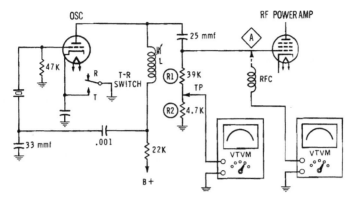

Fig. 8-3. Oscillator stage with output test point.

Test points are provided in some transmitters to permit easy connection of a test meter. Others have no designated test points. Nearly all can be tuned using only an RF power meter or lamp-type dummy load as a tune-up indicator.

A test point is provided in the grid circuit of the RF power amplifier to facilitate tune-up and checking of oscillator functioning in the circuit shown in Fig. 8-3. When a high-resistance DC voltmeter or DC VTVM is connected to test point TP, a reading between 0.7 to 2.0 volts (negative with respect to ground) is obtained when the oscillator is functioning properly. The test point is isolated from the RF path sufficiently by R1 to prevent mistuning of the oscillator tank (L) by the test meter and its leads. No voltage is present when the oscillator is not functioning.

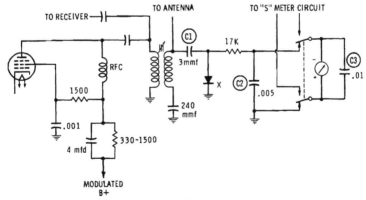

Fig. 8-4. RF power amplifier with RF output meter.

145

When such a test point is not provided, oscillator functioning in terms of RF power-amplifier grid drive can be measured by connecting a DC VTVM directly to the grid of the RF power-amplifier tube (point A in Fig. 8-3) through an RF choke or high-value resistor, as indicated by the dotted line. The reading will be higher than at the test point at the junction of the voltage divider.

Built-in RF output meter—A 0-1 DC milliammeter is built into the Courier 1 to serve as an RF power output meter when transmitting and an S meter when receiving. The transmitter output signal, as shown in Fig. 8-4, is fed through C1 to a rectifier-meter arrangement. Diode X short circuits positive-half RF signals to ground, leaving a negative DC voltage that is measured by the milliammeter and R which form a DC voltmeter. Capacitors C2 and C3 bypass any remaining RF to ground. The transmitter is tuned for maximum meter reading, and the meter serves as a handy reference for determining whether transmitter output is up to par.

When a transmitter is not equipped with an RF power-level meter, an external RF power meter with a built-in dummy antenna load, or a thru-line-type RF power meter terminated in a 50-ohm dummy load (instead of an antenna) is required for bench checking and tune-up of transmitters.

Ample grid drive, but insufficient power output, indicates that there is trouble in the RF-amplifier stage. This is possibly due to a defective tube, mistuning, or inadequate screen voltage resulting from a change in the value of the screen-voltage dropping resistor.

Neutralization

Neutralization is used in some CB transmitters to prevent self-oscillation by the RF power amplifier. The presence of an output signal with the transmitter crystal removed indicates that the RF power amplifier is oscillating. Neutralizing adjustments should be made in strict accordance with the set instruction book.

Low Modulation

The RF power meter indicates RF output when the transmitter is either modulated or not modulated. When modulated, the power-output indication should rise. The effective talk-power and range of the transmitter are seriously reduced when modulation level is inadequate. Methods for measuring modulation level are described in Chapter 4.

146

Inadequate modulation level can be caused by (1) improper use of the microphone; (2) insensitive or improperly matched microphone; (3) low plate voltage; (4) defective tube in modulator stage or preceding AF amplifier stages; or (5) defective component in the modulator system.

A modulator is simply an audio amplifier which applies a varying audio voltage in series with the plate and screen voltage applied to the RF power amplifier. Distorted audio is caused by the same defects as when distortion occurs in conventional audio amplifiers.

TROUBLESHOOTING CHART

Some manufacturers furnish excellent instruction books containing troubleshooting charts, voltage and resistance charts, and other information that makes servicing easier. Troubleshooting Chart 8-1 is based on one published by *e.c.i. electronic communications, inc.* in its *Courier 1* instruction book. It has been modified to be generally applicable to all CB sets.

Chart 8-1. Troubleshooting Procedures.

Entire Transceiver and Power Supply

Trouble	Probable Cause	Remedy
Pilot does not light.	No line voltage input. A. Blown fuse. B. Defective on-off switch.	Check voltages. Check for shorts and measure resistance as per resistance chart or schematic.
Rest of set is dead.	No B+1 voltage. A. Defective line filter capacitors. B. Defective vibrator/or buffer. C. Defective filter capacitors. D. Defective power transformer. E. Defective rectifier. F. Open filter resistor or choke.	Replace defective parts. Replace buffer also if vibrator is replaced.
Filaments do not light.	No AC or DC power input, blown fuses, or defective transformer. Defective line filters.	Check voltages and resistance. Replace parts found defective.
No sound from speaker. Cannot transmit. Pilot indicator O.K. Filaments O.K.	No plate voltage. Defect in power supply rectifier circuit. Short in B+ branch circuitry.	Check voltages and resistance. Replace parts found defective.
No B+	Bad rectifier, filters, open resistor or shorted buffer capacitor. (Open rectifier diodes cause low B+. Shorted rectifier diodes cause the power transformer to burn.)	Check voltages and resistance. Check rest of circuit for shorts. Replace defective parts.
In receive position. No sound. Power supply O.K. Modulator inoperative.	Defective speaker or output transformer. Defective part in modulator. Defective microphone "press to talk" switch.	Check voltages and resistances. Replace or repair defective components.

Chart 8-1 Troubleshooting Procedures (Cont'd.)

Intermittent	Tubes, shorts or broken wires due to vibration.	Check tubes by gently tapping. Make physical check for loose or broken wires. Make resistance check.
Excessive hum	Defective filters in power supply.	Check filters by substitution. Replace defective parts.
Dial calibration is off. (tunable receiver)	Dial may have been forced or turned. R.F. tracking off. (Must be reset if any frequency sensitive component has been replaced).	Reset dial. Realign receiver.
Meter needle sticks.	Meter face acquires static charge.	Discharge by wiping meter face with antistatic cloth.
Meter stays fully deflected or in zero position.	Defective related component. Zero adjust potentiometer shorted or open.	Check components for defects. Replace if defective.

Modulator

Trouble	Probable Cause	Remedy
Excessive hum pickup.	Wires from on-off switch to power supply pass too close to modulator. Defective microphone cord.	Dress wires under power supply close to chassis. Replace or repair cord.
Loud crackling noise from speaker.	Defective speaker voice coil shorting to ground.	Replace speaker.
Low or distorted audio. Low or distorted modulation.	Defective part in modulator. Defective microphone, defective modulation transformer or defective part in modulator.	Check tubes first, then make voltage and resistance checks to determine bad part. Replace defective components.

Receiver

Trouble	Probable Cause	Remedy
Fixed tune not working or erratic.	Defective wire from switch to crystals and/or trimmers. Defective fixed tune trimmers (if used).	Check wires and trimmers for shorts. Replace if defective.
Cannot tune high channels with fixed tune trimmers.	Trimmer capacitance excessive.	Add capacitor in series with trimmer and switch.
Burned Resistor	Defective capacitor or shorted or gassy tube.	Check tubes and capacitors. Replace bad parts.
Noise limiter ineffective or inoperative.	Defective diode or component in noise limiter circuit.	Check diode and components for voltage and resistance as per charts or schematic.
Receiver drift	Defective crystal.	Try new crystal.
R.F. interference	Tube shields missing.	Make certain tube shields are in place.
Adjacent channel interference.	Tuning of I.F. transformers too broad.	Realign receiver or consult manufacturer.

Chart 8-1 Troubleshooting Procedures (Cont'd.)

Interference from out-of-band station.	Inadequate rejection of strong out-of-band signals.	Construct and install wave trap at antenna input.
Short range	If set checks O.K., customer's antenna may be defective.	Check antenna, cable and connector.

Transmitter

Trouble	Probable Cause	Remedy
Cannot transmit Microphone and cord O.K.	Transmitter defective	Check tubes, voltages, resistance, and components for defect. Replace as necessary.
Low R.F. output.	Defective component in transmitter. Transmitter out of alignment.	Check tubes first, check alignment. Check for defective components. Make voltage and resistance checks. Replace defective parts.
Off-frequency	Defective transmit crystal. Defective oscillator tube. Crystal trimmer (if there is one) defective or out of alignment.	Check oscillator tube, crystal. If bad, replace. Replace or retune trimmer. Re-measure frequency.
Slow return of receiver after transmission.	Defective RF amplifier tube in receiver. Defective detector/AVC tube. Defective component in squelch circuit.	Check tubes. Check voltage and resistance. Replace bad parts.
Cannot transmit Receiver and transmitter O.K.	Microphone cord, switch, microphone or connector.	Check for defect. Repair or replace bad part.
Feedback (whistle type noise) while transmitting	Modulation transformer leads reversed during repair. Open capacitor across modulator transformer primary.	Check wiring. Replace capacitor.
Microphonics in receiver or transmitter.	Defective tubes.	Check all tubes by gently tapping to find microphonic tube.

SHOP CHECKOUT

Repair of CB sets is only part of the service technician's job. After repairs have been made to restore operation, a CB set should be given a complete check-out to make sure it delivers all of its original performance, and to make sure its performance complies with FCC requirements. The following check-out and service procedures are basic good practice.

Cleanliness

Dust and dirt inhibit cooling and cause leakage paths. Clean off accumulated foreign matter with a vacuum cleaner (not forced air) and a dry paint brush. When necessary, clean

149

parts with carbon-tet; but be careful, carbon-tet dissolves some kinds of insulating materials, corrodes some metals, and is poisonous to breathe. Clean relay and switch contacts with contact cleaning fluid—but never file them.

Tubes

Test all tubes with an accurate tube tester for shorts, merit (dynamic mutual conductance, transconductance or emission), grid emission, and interelectrode leakage. Replace all tubes that have any defects. Bear in mind that all tubes that pass muster on a typical tube tester will not necessarily perform adequately. Use the tube substitution method, if performance is not as rated, in addition to checking tubes with a tube tester.

Cables and Connectors

Inspect all cables for frayed insulation and loose strands of wire, as well as soldered connections at plugs. Replace worn cables and plugs. If the antenna connector does not match the plug on the customer's antenna coaxial cable, either install the proper type of plug or use an adaptor—make-shift coax connections lead to RF power losses.

Microphones

The microphone is the device into which the intended intelligence is fed. If the customer has an inadequate microphone, sell him a better one, but make sure its electrical characteristics match the set. Pay particular attention to push-to-talk switch contacts and microphone-cord shielding. Replace worn microphone cords; they are not expensive, and a new one can save a later (free) service call.

Power Supply

Replace vibrators whenever there is any doubt as to their continued reliability. Replace the buffer capacitor with one of the same value and same or higher voltage rating when replacing a vibrator. Electrolytic filter capacitors dry out. Replace them if they have been in service for two years or more.

Receiver Performance

Always check out a receiver for sensitivity and make sure that the receiver is as sensitive as its rating (usually less than

1 microvolt for 10 db signal-to-noise). Also, determine that the squelch opens with less than a microvolt input when set to best squelch sensitivity. Also, make sure that the squelch can be set so it won't open on normal noise.

While there is little you can do about improving selectivity, measure the selectivity and re-align the receiver if selectivity is not as good as rated.

While measuring sensitivity, increase the modulated RF signal input and make sure the full rated audio output is obtained without excessive distortion. AC voltage at speaker terminals should be equal to $\sqrt{WR}$ when W is the rated audio output in watts and R is the speaker impedance in ohms. Listen for audio output-level change as input signal is increased in order to determine that the AVC is working.

Listen for a decrease in ignition noise when the noise limiter is cut in. It should reduce noise but should not cause an excessive drop in speech level and *serious* introduction of distortion.

Using an accurate frequency meter, determine that all fixed-tuned receiving channels are "on the nose." Let the set operate for a while and recheck it to make sure it hasn't drifted.

If it's a tunable receiver, make sure you can tune in both channel 1 and channel 23.

Transmitter Performance

The customer looks to you to keep him out of trouble with the FCC in regard to transmitter performance. Measure the transmitter frequencies and replace the offending crystals if any channel is close to being off frequency by 0.005% (0.0025% is a better standard to go by). Recheck after letting the set run to determine whether any drift has taken place.

Measure power output with an RF power meter. If output is less than 2 watts, your customer may be dissatisfied. If it is over 3.5 watts, the FCC won't be happy. Also measure power input to the final RF power-amplifier stage if it can be done without undue inconvenience. Do this by measuring the plate voltage at the plate of the modulator tube (with the transmitter on and connected to an RF power meter and/or dummy load), and the RF power-amplifier cathode current. If means are provided for measuring RF power-amplifier plate current independently of screen current, determine its value. Then multiply the plate voltage by the measured current in amperes, and you'll get the answer in watts—it must be 5 watts or less.

Measure modulation with an oscilloscope and shop test receiver as described in Chapter 4. Make sure modulation is linear (equal up and down) and is above 70%, but never over 100%.

If the set has a TVI filter in the antenna circuit, turn on a TV set tuned to TV channel 2 and operate the transmitter. You will probably see an effect on the TV screen. Adjust the TVI filter for minimum effect on TV reception, or use a grid-dip meter and tune the filter to approximately 54 mc.

If there is no TVI filter and serious TV interference occurs, sell the customer a low-pass filter designed to cut off above 30-40 mc and for use in a 50-ohm unbalanced line. Connect it between the set antenna terminal and the antenna with a piece of coax fitted with appropriate plugs. Fasten the filter to the CB set chassis or case, making sure the filter case is securely grounded to the set.

Record Your Work

Keep a log and list the following facts about every set you service for reference:

1. Make, model, and serial number of set,
2. Name, address, and station call letters of set's owner,
3. Date on which set was serviced,
4. Signature of person servicing set,
5. Grade of operator license, and license expiration date, held by person servicing set or by person in charge who is responsible for the work done,
6. Repairs made; list of tubes and parts replaced,
7. Actual measured transmitter frequencies,
8. RF power output at all channels for which set is equipped,
9. Receiver sensitivity at all channels for which set is equipped,
10. Power input voltage applied when measurements were made.

If you wish to be a good salesman, attach a tag or sticker to the set noting the actual measured transmitter frequencies, date they were measured, and name of your company. This will help protect your customer if he gets an FCC citation for off-frequency operation and will remind him to call you when service is again required.

Chapter 9

Business Aspects of CB Servicing

With new station license applications flowing into the FCC at the rate of more than 12,000 per month, the CB servicing business has interesting potential. It is estimated that each station license application covers an average of three CB sets. This means that more than a million sets were in use in mid-1962 and that some 36,000 new sets are being sold monthly.

Most CB sets are sold by radio parts jobbers and mail order houses, which may or may not have service facilities. Citizens Radio specialty stores, on the other hand, generally maintain service departments. Many users go to professional two-way radio service shops when they experience trouble—others attempt to repair their own sets. The rapid growth of the CB radio market is causing many TV service shop operators to expand into CB servicing.

CB SERVICE SHOP

To get into the CB service business, adequate test equipment is required. While an unlicensed technician can service CB sets under certain conditions, a CB shop should employ at least one person holding a First-Class or Second-Class Radiotelephone Operator license. The licensed man is responsible for the work performed by unlicensed persons who work under his supervision. However, the technical work should not be difficult for a TV serviceman, since servicing TV sets requires more knowledge and skill than servicing transmitters. Therefore, to secure a part of the lucrative CB business, every TV serviceman should bend his efforts toward securing an FCC license.

The CB shop can participate in the multimillion dollar CB business by offering any or all of the following services:

1. Repair of CB sets for local radio-parts jobbers and local CB users,

2. Installation of CB sets for local radio-parts jobbers as well as those purchased from mail order houses,
3. Installation and sale of noise-suppression kits,
4. Installation and sale of CB accessories, improved antennas, lower-loss coaxial cable, etc.,
5. Installation and sale of CB sets directly to users,
6. Frequency-measuring service for local dealers and users.

The first step to take in getting into the CB service business is to get a radio operator's license. The next step is to get better informed about CB equipment by reading books and magazines. Instruction books on actual sets can often be obtained free of charge by writing directly to CB equipment manufacturers whose success depends on the availability of service on a local level.

Shop Equipment

Adequate test equipment is essential. A listing of the minimum test equipment required is given in Chapter 2. An investment of approximately $1,000 in test equipment is required. Two or three times that amount is required if laboratory-type equipment is selected.

Inventory

To profit from sales of antennas, a small inventory of various types of antennas, coaxial cable, and related hardware should be maintained. It will also be necessary to stock tubes, vibrators, and standard parts which can be purchased at local radio parts jobbers at wholesale prices by those who are in the legitimate CB service business. They are also available to everyone at advertised net prices from mail order houses.

It is not feasible to stock crystals unless many of the same makes and models are to be serviced. Crystals must be ground specifically for use in a particular set and are not interchangeable among various makes and models for CB sets. While a crystal ground for set A will work in set B, chances are that set B will not operate at the required frequency. Exact replacement parts and crystals must generally be purchased directly from CB equipment manufacturers, their distributors, or through their sales representatives serving your area.

To participate in sales of CB equipment, contact the manufacturers of your choice and advise them of your interest. Some brands may not be available to you due to prior arrangements for distribution in your area.

154

When buying CB equipment for resale, your cost often depends on the number of sets you want to buy. For example, one manufacturer allows a discount of 30% from suggested retail price when ordering in small quantities, and 40% when buying 50 or more sets at a time. However, you determine the price at which you sell the equipment. The advertised price is the "suggested" retail price and is not the price at which you are required to sell.

When selling antennas and other accessories, you are competing with mail order houses and other radio-parts jobbers who sell to the public at so-called wholesale prices. Some parts jobbers will sell only to established service shops and dealers, while others will sell at the same price as everyone else. If the volume of your purchases of accessories is great enough, you might be able to negotiate with a local parts jobber for lower prices so that you can offset competition from mail order houses and some parts jobbers.

Primarily, when engaging in the service business, you are selling services, and sales of equipment, parts, and accessories are secondary. Nevertheless, hardware sales can add significantly to your income.

SERVICE CHARGES

The rate you must charge for services depends on your costs and overhead. While a rate of $5 per hour is adequate in some areas, $10 per hour may not be enough in others. An equipment manufacturer must charge from $75 to $100 per day for the services of a field engineer or technician in order to defray out-of-pocket costs and overhead.

The following service charges are typical (not including material):

Install base station and antenna	$100.00
Install mobile unit and antenna on car	$ 25.00
Replace existing base-station antenna and coax	$ 50.00
Service call, base station, minimum charge	$ 10.00
Service call, mobile unit, minimum charge	
—car brought to shop	$ 7.50
—call at customer location	$ 10.00
Install noise suppression kit in car	$ 25.00
Install CB set and antenna on boat	$ 75.00
Frequency measurement—first channel	
—set brought to shop	$ 10.00
—at customer location	$ 15.00

Frequency measurement—

    additional channels each .... $ 2.50

Shop labor,

    —minimum charge .... $ 7.50

    —hourly rate .... $ 10.00

Complete check-out of set—at shop .... $ 25.00

Change frequency or replace crystals

    first channel .... $ 12.50

    additional channels, each .... $ 5.00

Commercial customers generally expect to be extended credit. If you don't know the customer's paying habits, it's a good idea to get bank references or subscribe to Dun & Brad-

REPAIR RATE SCHEDULE
LABOR AND PARTS
RAY-TEL CITIZENS BAND RADIOTELEPHONE
Model TWR-1

1   Raytheon will reimburse the Contractor for labor performed in the repair of defective In-Warranty Ray-Tel Citizens Band Radiotelephones (Model TWR-1), as follows

    A   MINOR REPAIRS $4 00

         Replacement of microphone, vibrator, tube, resistor, small capacitor, etc

    B   MAJOR REPAIRS $5 00

         Replacement of I F , audio, or power transformer, speaker, electrolytic capacitor, couplate, control, switch, alignment, etc

    NOTE

         The amounts shown above include bench work, and the removal and reinstallation of equipment in vehicle if such is necessary, and constitute the maximum amounts which Raytheon will pay for labor in either category Repair jobs will fall into category "A" or "B" and may not be combined A maximum of $5 00 will be paid to the Contractor for labor charges for any repair job performed under this Agreement

2   Raytheon will reimburse the Contractor for replacement parts used in the repair of defective In-Warranty Ray-Tel Citizens Band Radiotelephones (Model TWR-1), as follows

    A   Parts which are specialized to this equipment, per Appendix A, and which have been purchased from Raytheon will be credited at the prices listed, less 40% In addition a 10% handling and stocking charge will be allowed

    B   Parts which are commonly found in other equipments of this nature, Appendix B, are normally replaceable at no charge through local procurement sources, however, if the Contractor is forced to pay for these replacement parts, Raytheon will credit the Contractor at established industry list prices, less 40% In addition a 10% handling and stocking charge will be allowed

3   Contractor should invoice Raytheon for the above labor and parts on "In-Warranty Claim" Form No DL-7077 Claim submitted on other than this form will not be honored

4   All defective in-warranty parts for which Raytheon is billed must be tagged with a Defective Parts Tag (Form No DL-7078) and held in stock for sixty (60) days pending disposition instructions from Raytheon

5   Prior to performing no-charge in-warranty service on this equipment, the Contractor is expected to verify and to certify that the equipment is within Raytheon's 90-day warranty period, in accordance with the current applicable Service Policy and Procedure

    Please Note

    a   This Schedule covers only shop repairs, including removal and installation of equipment in vehicle, but specifically excludes any allowance for travel time, service calls, transportation charges, etc Responsibility for all such charges are to be assumed by the individual or company requesting service

    b   This Schedule is subject to change if at any time it appears to be inequitable to Raytheon or the Contractor In the event of any such change, Raytheon will notify the Contractor thirty (30) days prior to the effective date of change

DL 7082

Courtesy Raytheon Co.

Fig. 9-1. Sample repair-rate schedule.

street credit information service. Many commercial customers will be interested in having their equipment serviced on a contract basis. Typically, the charge for maintaining a base station is $25 per month and $10 per mobile unit, material included. For this the customer is entitled to one preventive maintenance call per month and unlimited emergency service during normal business hours.

Some manufacturers arrange with independent service shops to handle maintenance during the warranty period. Typical rates are shown in Fig. 9-1 and a typical report form is shown in Fig. 9-2.

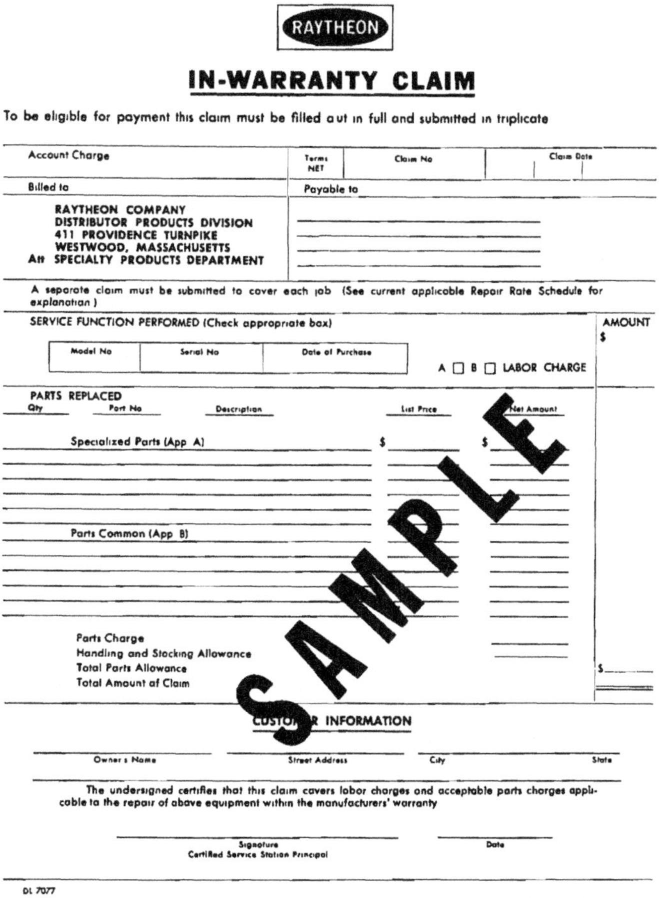

Courtesy Raytheon Co.

Fig. 9-2. Sample in-warranty claim form.

PROMOTING CB SERVICE BUSINESS

You can succeed in the CB service business only if you let your prospective customers know that your services are available. Your markets include local CB set users, local distributors of CB equipment, and manufacturers and distributors who sell equipment in your area by mail.

To reach local CB set users, you can advertise your services in local newspapers and on local radio stations, as well as at your place of business and on your service vehicles. You can mail announcements to local CB set users by looking them up in a Citizens Band call book. You might also advise the FCC office nearest you that your services are available to those who inquire about local CB set service. A personal call on all radio parts jobbers in your area may produce subcontract service work, or referrals of service calls to you.

By all means, write to CB equipment manufacturers and tell them about your availability and qualifications. Kit manufacturers and mail order houses might also be happy to know of the availability of your services in case of need.

When doing a large volume of business, it may pay to have spare sets available for use as *loaners*. To meet the requirements of all customers, the spare sets should be of the type that are operable on all 23 channels (crystal controlled transmit and receive). Thus, it will not be necessary to install crystals for a customer's frequency since these sets can be set to any channel without modification.

You can also rent CB sets. However, renters must have their own station license—they may not legally use a rented set without a license, or under your license. Typical rental charge for a set selling for $230 is as follows:

One day $15
One week $35
One month $75
One year .... $20 per month
Five years .... $10 per month

For these rental fees, you should be able to handle maintenance without additional charge, if the customer brings the sets to your shop for service, or if you furnish loaners while repairs are being made. Since costs vary, you should consult your accountant or bank when establishing rental rates. When leasing equipment on an annual or longer term basis, your bank may be willing to purchase your lease contract and free your money for other purposes.

Index

CPSIA information can be obtained
at www.ICGtesting.com
Printed in the USA
BVOW06*0718230317
479199BV00012B/21/P